EDUCATION TOWARD ADULTHOOD

Education Toward Adulthood

GABRIEL MORAN

PAULIST PRESS
New York/Ramsey/Toronto

Published by Paulist Press
Editorial Office: 1865 Broadway, New York, N.Y. 10023
Business Office: 545 Island Road, Ramsey, N.J. 07446

Printed and bound in the
United States of America

Contents

Introduction   1

1. A Revolution Delayed   3

2. Meanings of Adulthood   17

3. An Educational Model   37

4. Religious Journey to Adulthood   56

5. The Family in Educational Context   82

6. Forms of Learning   105

7. Professionalism: Friend or Foe?   130

Conclusion   150

Introduction

This book attempts to provide some theoretical material for the religious education of adults. In the last decade publishers have brought out many books on procedures and programs for adult education in churches. These materials have been helpful to many people in their work. However, my interest in this book lies elsewhere. I think there is a need to examine the philosophical underpinnings and the educational models of the adult education movement. I will distinguish, for example, between adult education and the education of adults as well as between the education of adults and education toward adulthood. Important philosophical choices can be reflected in these linguistic distinctions.

This book is unabashedly theoretical. But there are two distinct meanings of the word "theory." In one case someone devises a plan or theory for the way the world should look. After that someone else is supposed to "implement" the theory or put it into practice. Sometimes this kind of theorizing may help, but it is rightfully suspect in many quarters today. Such theory can actually create further obstacles to productive activity.

In the other meaning of "theory," one begins from within practice and uses language to describe what people are already doing. With the aid of a few key distinctions, people may come to see better why they are doing what they are doing and how they might shift their efforts.

This book is theory in the second sense. Everything referred to in this book already exists. There are no proposals to invent organizations that would be entirely new or to start acting in ways that have never been tried. Theory, in the sense I am appealing to, has as its direct aim the modest hope of helping people see possibilities which they had overlooked because they lacked names for their experiences. This modest hope, however, is tied to a truly radical possibility, namely, that as people better describe their experience, the world is transformed beyond what any theory makers could envision.

I hope that there are two groups in particular who will find this book useful. For people whose job is adult education in churches, I am trying to provide models for testing existing programs. Many of these people are working heroically with small resources. Some of the principles in this book may imply a critical judgment on the programs they are running. In the main, however, I would hope to be supporting them in directions they are already taking.

There is another audience with whom I work and to whom this book is addressed. These people may or may not be church members. Often they have tried church programs, but did not stay. They have a sense of what an adult and religious education ought to be. They are frustrated not just by the churches but by public education as well. Despite frustrations they do not give up hope or quit working for something better. I am both drawing upon their experience and also trying to give it articulate form. I hope that this book will help them in seeing the issues clearly and organizing their efforts efficiently to improve education for all of us.

1. A Revolution Delayed

Since the turn of this century there have been regular announcements by writers, conventions, and institutions that "adult education" is finally coming into its own. Something called "adult education" can be traced back much farther than the end of the last century. But the conscious and articulated movement named "adult education" is largely a phenomenon of the twentieth century. The movement is worldwide in extent and it includes, sometimes quite prominently, religious institutions.

The question I wish to examine in this book is why the adult education movement never does seem to arrive. Statistics to be cited seem to me unambiguous; neither worldwide nor in the United States has "adult education" fulfilled its promise. Within this context I wish to ask two further questions. First, what significance does this always coming but never arriving movement have for the Christian churches? Second, what significance do churches have in any movement for the education of adults?

The "adult education" movement made its first impact between the world wars. Growth has continued up through the 1970s. Books on "adult education" can now cite impressive statistics on the number of people participating in programs. Other writers, however, who are looking critically at the needs of the nation are skeptical about the significance of those numbers.[1]

At the worldwide level the contrast between the apparent success (i.e., growth) of "adult education" and the inadequacy of what has so far been achieved is striking. After surveying the rapid expansion of "adult education," John Lowe concludes: "If adult education facilities continue to expand at the same rate as over the past 15 years, gratifying though that rate has been, then the gap between needs and fulfillment will steadily widen."[2] Adult education, in short, is taking one step when it needs two to keep even. Without belittling anyone's efforts it must still be asked whether more steps forward will solve or even ameliorate the situation. If the problem were that adult education's arrival is simply taking longer than had been expected, then patience and continued exertion would be the appropriate remedy. But if, as admitted by the movement's advocates, the effect of adult education is to widen the world's gaps—educationally, culturally, economically—then some rethinking of basic concepts is called for.

There have been three international congresses of "adult education": Elsinore, Denmark (1948), Montreal, Canada (1960), and Tokyo, Japan (1972). The Tokyo conference attracted four hundred delegates from eighty-two countries. In contrast to the Montreal meeting which was composed largely of adult educators, the Tokyo meeting was heavily weighted with administrators and politicians. The composition of the congress perhaps explains the direction it took. John Lowe writes of the meeting: "The desirability of lifelong education was no longer a controversial topic; controversy was centered upon the methods by which lifelong education might be instituted during the adult phase of life."[3]

Lowe thinks that this direction to the meeting was a hopeful sign. Everybody is agreed that lifelong education is a good thing; now it remains to put lifelong education into practice. However, much of what came from that meeting and much that comes from other sources belie the apparent agreement.

"Lifelong education" is a phrase coined for popular usage only in the 1960s. No one is likely to attack "lifelong education." Who could be against such a nice idea? Nevertheless, one is bound to suspect that what everybody immediately agrees upon is likely to be innocuous. "Lifelong education" might be better off as a controversial topic than as a general piety.

The hard statistics which UNESCO gathered before the Tokyo meeting support this suspicion. Most countries of the world had fewer than one hundred people identifiable as "adult educators." Of thirty-nine countries responding to the UNESCO survey, nineteen were devoting less than 1 percent of their educational budget to "adult education"; only four countries were devoting as much as 3 percent.[4] How does one reconcile these economic realities with the supposed agreement on the value of "lifelong education"? If the people who used to talk about "adult education" are now the ones who talk of "lifelong education," the rhetoric may have become more general, but the economic picture may remain unchanged.

My attention in this book will be directed to the United States but within a worldwide context. Concerning oneself with the richest country of the world may seem uncalled for in light of the point just made. I limit my scope to the United States for two reasons. The first is that the United States is the place I know best. The task of writing from other and wider perspectives I leave to people who are competent for the job. A second reason is that a change in the United States could help the poor of the world. I do not refer simply to the amount of money which the United States gives in direct grants. The percentage of its wealth that the United States gives to poor countries bears a peculiar resemblance to the percentages which governments allocate to "adult education." That tiny percentage might be enlarged in both cases, but there is also need for a reconceptualization of both questions.

In the short run poor countries may need money from the United States. During coming decades a change in the self-image of the United States is what would benefit poor countries. Educators in the United States have to work for a change in the nation's use of natural resources and its relation to smaller and poorer countries. Education toward adulthood is a way of approaching the question of United States power. If persons, groups, and the nation itself became more adult, then the rest of the world would have a better chance.

The United States has always been intensely committed to education, especially in the form of schools. Part of the American dream which the United States took to itself was to provide opportunity for all its people to share in self-government and wealth. Only through education, it was supposed, could that dream come true. Thomas Jefferson continually returned to this theme: "We hope to avail the state of those talents which Nature has sown as liberally among the poor as among the rich, but which perish without use."[5]

The American dream, said James Adams, is "that dream of a land in which life should be better and richer and fuller for every man, with opportunity for each according to his ability or achievement."[6] The United States has had a mixed record of success in reaching this ideal. The country has proved to be a land of opportunity for millions of people. For other people, especially nonwhites, and for many women the success story has been less spectacular. But when the ideal has not been reached, a still greater commitment to the schools has been called for. The reason for that is obvious in Adam's definition. "Life should be better and richer and fuller" logically applies to one's children even more than to oneself. Thus, the American dream could always be turned over to the school and its children. True, the dream has not been reached yet, but be patient; the next generation will have it. And what is the means to success? A standard answer has been: universal, free, compulsory education in schools.[7]

With "child education" so enthusiastically endorsed in the United States one could possibly guess the fate of "adult education." If child education was to prepare people for success in adult life, who were these people still looking for education when they were adults? The answer is: the "failures" of that system. The "adult education" market would be immigrants unschooled in the English language, poor men who were at the bottom of the economic pile despite schooling, and women who were outsiders to the system simply because they were women.

Statistics on "adult education" confirm this expectation. The major study of the participants and courses in "adult education" was done in the 1960s.[8] At that time one-third of all courses were in vocational training; one-fifth of courses were in areas of leisure and cultural activity. Although men and women were participants of programs in about equal numbers, the men completely dominated the vocational courses while the women were the great majority in leisure/cultural courses.[9]

Rich and successful men were not in "adult education." They received their education and then went up the ladder of success. At the other end of the spectrum poor women could not think of "adult education." They were struggling to survive at home or else caught in jobs that needed no training. Thus, the market for "adult education" turns out to be a peculiar combination: poor men and rich women. To this day "adult education" still rests on these two radically different bases of the nineteenth century.

"Adult education" has always been praised in the United States. Who could think of opposing it? On the one side it provided hope, uplifting, and control for poor men. On its other side it was an outlet for upper-class women. High rhetoric, however, does not pay the bills. "Adult education" has always been hopelessly underfinanced. As a competitor in the free market, it has never been able to pay its way.

Timothy Claxton, writing in 1826, describes the great success of the Boston Mechanics Institute: "It became evident that in Boston, as well as in other places, it only required a little exertion on the part of those who felt an interest in the subject to induce at least a portion of its citizens to improve those advantages." Nonetheless, the next paragraph of his essay includes the statement that "receipts were found insufficient to defray the expenditures and the lectures were discontinued."[10] The level of financial sophistication in nineteenth-century "adult education" can also be seen in a stipulation of John Lowell. At his institute a lecturer could receive a small sum from each scholar "not exceeding the value of two bushels of wheat for the course of six months."[11] One should hardly be surprised that a stable faculty was difficult to find if that arrangement was typical of their financial security.

"Adult education" in the nineteenth and twentieth centuries has been badly lacking any institutional base of power. The obvious institution for the education of adults would seem to be the university. Universities have buildings, people, and money; furthermore, at least by some criteria, they are already in the business of educating adults. However, universities have traditionally taken a very restricted segment of the adult population as their major concern.

In recent decades colleges and universities have made efforts to reach a wider population. Often, however, the university simply adds programs which are in continuity with the past of "adult education." That is, some poor men and some middle- and upper-class women are reached with "extension services" from the university. The main operations of the university continue with business as usual and the vast majority of adults remains untouched.

I would not belittle university efforts to reach out to people in more ways. But not every addition is progress unless conceptual and linguistic improvements are made. The concept of "adult education" carries a well defined but narrow meaning. In 1926 Eduard Lindeman worried that the United States would discover "adult education" and that it would be successful because of "advertising psychologists and supersalesmen." "The chief danger which confronts adult education," wrote Lindeman, "lies in the possibility that we may 'Americanize' it before we understand its meaning."[12]

The United States's system of education has been devoted almost exclusively to children. "Adult education" has been a tiny operation tacked on to the system. We in the United States tend to suppose that if we have built something too small, we can with our resources and technical skill simply enlarge it. The United States could therefore quickly develop master's and doctoral programs in seventy-five universities. By 1971 there were over one thousand doctors of "adult education" in the United States. Although these figures represent progress of one kind, some questions still have to be raised. The full-fledged development of a field called "adult education" may not be the best way to meet the needs of adults and children, women and men, rich and poor in the United States.

Two parallel cases suggest a comparison to the concept of "adult education." I would like to examine black education and women's education. In the history of the United States, education has been mainly a white affair. Black people and other racial minorities have not fared anywhere near so well. From the first years of the nation's existence, Jefferson and others agonized over discrimination against blacks. The development of black schools went a small way in rectifying the situation. Later the addition of "black studies" to existing universities might make people aware of the problem and be a symbolic commitment to the future. Such programs could never be a solution to the question of education for black people.

Starting in the 1950s the country had to admit that a doctrine of a separate but equal system for blacks was a charade. Not that there is anything impossible about a separate system being an equal system. But in this case the resources were so completely entrenched on one side that all historical efforts to build something comparable on the other side were futile. Furthermore, equality may not be an adequate ideal here. The word "equality" does not describe a system in which whites and blacks would make unique contributions as they worked together. However long the journey may take, we need an educational system which includes blacks and whites; we also need curricula in which black concerns are evident. A "black studies" program may at times be useful but only within a system that has accepted black into its mainstream. Whatever transitional ambiguities exist, whites would also be better off in such an integrated system.

A second relevant example is the sexual bias of United States education. Here too the pattern has existed from the start of the country. Education was conceived and institutionalized as a way to widen the choices of every little boy. Any boy might grow up to be President or do any line of work he chose. Some early voices, especially that of Benjamin Rush, were raised in support of universal education for women.[13] But whereas education for boys was intended to widen their possibilities, the education of girls was directed toward their accepting a sex-specific role. The Rev. John Ogden could say in all seriousness: "Every woman is born with an equal right to be the wife of the most eminent man."[14] The nineteenth century saw the blossoming of a system of women's colleges and finishing schools. While many of these schools and colleges were of high intellectual quality, their efforts were limited by preexisting assumptions in the society.

In recent times women took a page from the black revolution and demanded "women's studies" in universities. The limitations of this approach are as obvious as in the case of black studies. Unless everything that is not "women's studies" is considered "men's studies," then the addition of women's studies has made little impact. Unless "women's studies" receives power and money equal to "men's studies," then women would remain an attachment to the main business of the university. A separate but equal system is not likely to occur and, as is the case with black education, an equal system for women is not the ideal. What is needed is a sexually integrated system in which women and men can each make unique contributions. Women have therefore begun working to integrate the faculty and student body of schools while examining the entire curriculum for sexual bias.

The case of "adult education" is, I would suggest, a similar issue. Everyone can speak positively about it and then attach it to the main business of existing institutions. People who are interested in the education of adults may accept the deal because it seems to be a step in the right direction. The statistics I have cited might be interpreted otherwise. Even if "adult education" gets to be 1 percent of the budget of university or national policy, it will be reaching only a minute part of the adult population.

The parallel of adult to blacks and women is not an accident. The clientele of "adult education" has been drawn from poor blacks and other minorities on the one side and women on the other side. A movement for the education of adults should be inclusive of black and feminist concerns. Like blacks and feminists, educators who wish to see education open to all people all of their lives cannot be content with an "adult education" department in universities.

The development of an academic field of "adult education" must therefore be viewed with some suspicion. Since it must move against the tide of education, its twin dangers are that it will be insignificant in its impact or polemical in its approach. When "adult education" becomes a complete system with its own buildings, budget, personnel, and textbooks, it is clear that there is a distinct entity. But the rest of education continues on its course. "Adult education" may be cheerfully allowed existence as an independent but insignificant branch of education.

No one likes to be bracketed as insignificant. When "adult

education" sees itself in that position, it can easily turn polemical. Since it is the part of education which is called "adult," it may mistake the child as its opponent. "Adult education" can find itself in the position of suggesting that there is something undesirable about the education of children. If the conceptual scheme separates child and adult, then every dollar given to the child is a dollar taken from the adult. One therefore hears the cry from "adult education" that the United States is too interested in the education of children, a dangerous statement that will help neither adult nor child.

The doubtful value of a field called "adult education" can be illustrated with the word "teacher." A frequent statement in adult education literature is that we should be concerned with learning not teaching. Anyone seeing that contrast for the first time would probably be puzzled. Of course education should be concerned with learning. But why speak as if the great obstacle to learning were teaching? The answer is that "adult education" in order to be a separate field defines itself against the system of child, school, and teacher. The trouble with this tactic is that it gives over all the ordinary, rich, and ancient words to the other side. Then one is forced either to create an artificial jargon or to use ordinary language even as one attacks it. The case is so well known that I don't think it is necessary to demonstrate that "adult education" is afflicted by an expansive jargon.

The other result is more subtle and more important. In reference to teacher, "adult education" constantly snipes at the word but inevitably falls back into using it. The resulting confusion blocks any clear analysis. For example, in the Final Report of the Tokyo conference we read on page 14: "In adult education practice it was now widely accepted that the concepts of 'student' and 'teacher' were inadequate. Instead of 'teacher' the words 'guide' or 'counselor' or '*animateur*' were increasingly being used."[15] Fair enough, one might say; perhaps "adult education" can succeed without the word "teacher." However, on page 35 of the same report we read: "Adult education should be treated in the syllabus of teacher-training courses. Their curricula should include such topics as the psychology of the adult learner, community problems and training methods and techniques."[16] This demand has no ground to stand on. If one gives up on the words "teacher" and "teaching" for adults, one should not be surprised that teacher-training courses do not include methods for teaching adults.

I am citing the word "teacher" here as one crucial example of the double edge in any separate system of "adult education." Should one speak of school as if it were a child's word or should one work to open school to people of every age? Should one forever carry a stereotype of teacher as authoritarian master or should one rehabilitate the verb "to teach" as a good that any human being might do for another. The choice of words here determines our images of education and institutional policies.

I am obviously casting my vote for a rehabilitation of the old and rich words.[17] That choice is based upon the continuity of the child's world and the adult's world. There are emphases which shift from age to age where education is concerned. But "adult education" set over against "child education" creates two crude stereotypes. There is no such thing as "the adult learner" any more than there is a "child learner." There are many stages of adulthood just as there is variety in childhood. The learning patterns of children and adults are influenced by many things besides age.

Two distinct but related issues concern me in the chapters that follow: 1) How do we reach far more adults than "adult education" reaches? The answer will be educational patterns that include children as well as adults; 2) How do we devise an educational system that educates toward "adulthood," an ideal to be examined in the next chapter. Here too a system educating toward adulthood includes both children and adults.

The final concern of this chapter is the relationship of religion and education. For discussing this relation of religion and education I return to the examples in the last section. Religion in the United States has had similar problems with education as have had blacks, women, and adults. That is, religion has been discriminated against in the public sector of education. The United States as the child of Western Enlightenment has never conceived of religion as something that intelligent people would discuss in public.

Religion, to be sure, has been the recipient of high praise and careful tolerance. Jefferson, Franklin, and other founders knew the practical importance of religion in the nation's life. Their chief concern was to see that religion did not become divisive in the public domain. Everyone was encouraged to have any religion he or she wanted but to practice it in the privacy of home and church. When an extensive system of public schools was established in the nineteenth century, the possibility of religious conflicts was carefully excluded. The writing of Horace Mann is explicit on the point. A "common religion" underlay the existence of the schools, but anything that smacked of "sects," "tenets," or "revealed truth" was to be avoided.[18]

Faced with an educational system that was "secular," what could religious groups do? They could follow the twofold approach adopted by blacks and women. First, try adding your own religious schools. Second, try adding religion to the secular school. Both approaches have been tried and are still being tried. In the nineteenth century the Protestant Sunday School and the Catholic parochial school were impressive complements to the public school. In the twentieth century there is a movement to add "religious studies" to the curriculum of public schools.

These two correctives are helpful steps. They also keep alive the question of religion and education. The limitations, however, are the same as in the case of blacks, women, and adults. A separate but equal system of religious schools is not likely and probably not desirable. A course on religion in elementary and secondary schools does not provide leverage to examine the place of religion in education and life. Adding a religion course to the existing form of education is only a small part of providing a genuine religious education for all citizens. The aim should be an educational system in which people could acquire greater understanding and deeper appreciation of religion throughout their whole lives.

The parallel I have drawn in relating adult education and religious education raises an intriguing question. Is there an intrinsic reason for this parallel or is there simply a vague and accidental similarity here? Another way to put the question is: Do adult and religious offer a similar challenge to the concept and institutionalization of education? I pointed out the reason why

adult in relation to education paralleled black and women's education. But how are adult and religious related both historically and
conceptually?

The historical question here is the possibility that "adult
education" has failed to arrive because it has never sufficiently
incorporated the religious element in adult lives. Nineteenth-
century efforts in educating adults were often allied with religious
motivation and institutions.[19] As the movement matured, however, religion seemed to become less important. True, there are
still courses on religion in "adult education" programs, but they
are relatively few in number and are almost entirely under the
sponsorship of church and synagogue.[20] The bigger issue of how
religion is related to human experience and especially the significance of religion in the lives of older adults is difficult to find in
the literature of "adult education."

The conceptual possibility I am suggesting is that there may
be a natural alliance between adulthood (or some conception of
adulthood) and religion (at least some form of religiousness). If
that is so, then these two allies have hardly been introduced to
each other in the educational system. They are together in
church-sponsored programs, but there may not be enough room
there to explore the full range of adult religiousness. Furthermore, if "adult religious education" is given over exclusively to
churches, the dominant educational system can easily dismiss the
question of religion and adulthood.

The time is ripe for a challenge to the meaning of education in
our society both from a concern for religion and from a concern
for adulthood. New alliances might be possible today that would
have been unthinkable in the nineteenth century. Our educational
system tends to exclude adults and religion. The need is to open
that system to the concerns which all people have throughout all
their lives.

This project is not a new one, but the United States is at an
interesting and important crossroads on these matters. The
United States is no longer young nor is its population mainly
youth.[21] Today there are new critical studies of blacks, of women,
and of the family. The last decade has produced new studies of
public education. The United States seems ready to come into its

own as an ecumenical center for all religions. Never in our history have there been such rich resources with which to respond to the question: What direction should our educational system take to help us all to grow up to better lives? Never has it been more important to the United States and to the world of nations that we answer that question.

Notes

1. See Willard Wirtz, *The Boundless Resource* (Washington, New Republic, 1975), p. 9.

2. John Lowe, *The Education of Adults: A World Perspective* (Paris, UNESCO, 1975), p. 216.

3. *Ibid.*, p. 14.

4. *Ibid.*, p. 132.

5. Quoted in Henry S. Commager, *The Empire of Reason* (New York, Anchor, 1977), p. 125.

6. Quoted in Horace Kallen, *Philosophical Issues in Adult Education* (Springfield, Charles C. Thomas, 1962), p. 50.

7. See Kenneth Keniston, *All Our Children: The American Family under Pressure* (New York, Harcourt, 1977), p. 41; David Tyack, "Ways of Seeing: An Essay in the History of Compulsory Schooling," *Harvard Educational Review*, 46(1976), p. 367.

8. See John Johnstone, *Volunteers for Learning* (Chicago, NORC, 1963).

9. *Ibid.*, pp. 78, 45.

10. Quoted in C. Hartley Grattan, *American Ideas about Adult Education 1760–1951* (New York, Teachers College, 1959), p. 20.

11. *Ibid.*, p. 40.

12. Eduard Lindeman, *The Meaning of Adult Education* (New York, New Republic, 1926), p. xix.

13. Benjamin Rush, *Thoughts on Female Education* (Philadelphia, 1787).

14. Quoted in Nancy Cott, *The Bonds of Womanhood: 'Woman's Sphere' in New England 1780–1835* (New Haven, Yale, 1977), p. 109.

15. UNESCO, *Third International Conference: Final Report* (Paris, UNESCO, 1972).

16. *Ibid.*

17. Martin Buber, *The Knowledge of Man* (New York, Harper and Row, 1965), p. 115.

18. See Horace Mann, *The Republic and the School*, ed. Lawrence Cremin (New York, Teachers College, 1957).

19. See Grattan, *op. cit.*, p. 48.

20. Johnstone, *op. cit.*, p. 64, found that 96 percent of religion courses were sponsored by church and synagogue.

21. At the beginning of the United States the median age was about 16; today that age would have more than doubled. See Current Population Reports, U.S. Department of Commerce, Bureau of the Census, *Demographic Aspects of Aging and the Older Population in the U.S.*, Special Studies Series, no. 59 (Washington, U.S. Government Printing Office, 1976), p. 23.

2. Meanings of Adulthood

The title of this chapter as well as the title of this book uses the word "adulthood." At first sight the word may appear unambiguous enough. Everyone has a fairly good idea of what is meant by adulthood. Or do they? Since this book describes education as a movement toward adulthood, we have to be clear about the meaning of this goal.

As a beginning clarification, there is a difference between "adult" used to designate an age and "adult" used as a psychological or social description. In the first or chronological sense people are called "adult" whenever they reach some stipulated age. A chronological meaning of adult is usually part of a legal system. Secular law in the West has never tried to define adulthood but only to decide at what age one is an adult.[1]

Chronological age is a very clear category, but there is no agreement on which is the year that distinguishes child from adult. As far back as Blackstone's *Commentaries* (1765), which were so influential in the United States, there has been acknowledgment that one became an adult at different ages for different things.[2] This ambiguity remains a part of contemporary society. A person might inherit wealth at 21 but be able to vote at 18. In many places one can drive a car at 16; in the 1960s the recording industry began defining adult as 14 or older.

The second meaning of "adult" is more difficult to tie down. It implies a psychosocial ideal and therefore something desirable. Although this usage of adult or adulthood is very common today, it is actually a recent invention. As of 1968 the *International*

17

Encyclopedia of the Social Sciences had articles on "aging" and "adolescence" but none on "adulthood."[3] Obviously, the writers of the encyclopedia recognized that there was a condition called "adult," but its status as a concept of the social sciences was apparently not clear at all. Only in this century has an ideal of adulthood been distinguished from chronological adulthood and systematically examined. "We have moved, over the years, from condition to process. In our culture, adulthood as a condition used to be simply assumed; as a process, it now seems to demand explanation."[4]

Most people, if they reflect on the matter, recognize these two meanings of "adult." They can see that these two meanings are constantly used in conversation and writing. What may not be so obvious is that these two meanings overlap in ways that can be confusing. In this book I will regularly use "adult" as a noun in referring to the fact of a chronological stage. I will use "adult" as an adjective to describe experiences, institutions, and persons with a distinctive quality to be defined in this chapter. When a corresponding noun is needed for adult as a psychosocial ideal, I will use "adulthood." My choices here are not wholly arbitrary. Common speech reflects this distinction between chronological adults and acting in an adult way. As might be expected, common speech is not always consistent in this usage.

The inconsistency and ambiguity find their way into educational writing. Church people refer these days to the "adult community." Does that phrase mean a community with the quality of adulthood or a community of grownups? It would appear that often the user is not aware that there are two meanings, let alone have thought through their relation. If church documents today say that "adult baptism" should be the norm, this phrase can mean two things: *a)* grownups are the ones for whom baptism is generally intended; *b)* an ideal of adulthood should guide the baptism of children and adults.[5]

Does "adult education" mean education of a certain quality or education of people who are not children? Historically, the two things have been confusedly related. Clearly, "adult education" has meant the education of people who are not children. When that question is at issue, we would do better to refer to the "education of adults." Otherwise, when "adult education" is used, there is also implied in the term a meaning of adulthood that is left unquestioned.

"Adult education" acquired its twentieth-century meaning within an economic and institutional setting that governed the meaning of the adjective "adult." "Adult education" came to refer to that small part of the population who were to receive the education. "Adult education" also implied what that part of the population was to be educated for. Those people who did not have institutional slots were to be given a way to fit. If the ideal of adulthood remains unexamined, then "adult education" will function to fit people into the existing slots. Those who manage machines may be better off than those who operate the machines, but both groups will be dominated by a restricted meaning of adulthood. That is the reason for Karl Marx's paradoxical statement that "in a capitalist society no one is (an) adult."

I have already introduced a further distinction in addition to that between "adult" as chronological fact and "adult" as psychosocial idea. Within the adjective "adult" there can be some radical differences of opinion. Within United States society there are two strongly contrasting ideals in the use of adult as a quality of personal life. I think that the less adequate one tends to dominate the discussion of adulthood. The difficult step is getting to the point where these two ideals are recognized and people can see that there is a questionable ideal of adulthood which controls our myths, institutions, and reform movements.

I have now suggested three meanings of adult in contemporary uses of the term. I shall presently add a fourth and look at the meanings and their interrelationship. Before that, however, I wish to point out the key that helped me to see these different meanings of adult and the inadequacy of the one that dominates our culture. The key was old people. It struck me that the meaning we often give to adult implicitly excludes old people. If our society is supposedly set up "to produce adults" and yet people can, as it were, grow out of adulthood, then both our society and its old people would be in trouble.

One frequently sees the statement that there are three parts to life: child, youth, adult. The statement could simply be a description of chronological fact except that certain characteristics are regularly connected with each of the three categories. Thus, children are supposed to play, youth to study, and adults to work. This description might not be so bad either except it is also assumed that adults retire from work when they reach a certain age. If one has been (an) adult, that is, a worker, but is no longer working, what does one become? Artificial categories (e.g., senior citizen) cannot hide an attitude of condescension. The person became an adult but is no longer an adult. The simple fact is that old age is an insoluble problem for our image of what it means to be adult. Children can grow up, women can be liberated, criminals can be rehabilitated. But there is nothing one can do to "re-adult" the old. The closer to death one moves the more obvious becomes the terrible flaw in our common meaning of acting adult.

The question was crystallized for me in a book by John Dunne, *A Search for God in Time and Memory*.[6] Here as in much of his writing, Dunne meditates on the significance of death in the human search for life's meaning. In most descriptions of life there are three parts to life's journey: the child, the youth, and the adult. "Perhaps," writes Dunne, "we could actually say that there are four metamorphoses if we count the child at the beginning as well as the child at the end. . . . This would mean that what is ordinarily called 'second childhood' is a kind of parody of what the old man can be."[7] Dunne is using childhood here to describe a fourth stage. This stage circles back to the beginning and calls into question what we have "grown up" to in the second and third stages. Do we in fact ever grow up and leave childhood behind us? The end of life puts the whole process in question.

Between the first and fourth stages there is a similarity which allows the word "child" to be used for both. However, the child at the end "is autonomous by appropriating his entire life, by accepting both the period of his alienation and that of his autonomy, both the period of his dependency and that of his independence. He says *yes* to his life and is willing to live the entire thing once more."[8]

I don't wish to endorse without reservation the language of

this description (I am not certain the language is Dunne's final position since he is commenting on Nietzsche in the passage quoted). What does strike me is that assumptions about growing up to be adult in our society are seriously threatened by old people in the same society. Psychology books often seem to be saying that people should become self-directing individuals who increasingly grow away from dependence on others. Of course, such books never deny that people get old and die. However, that fact is attached as a coda instead of being an interpretive key to the rest of life. The implied movement is a straight line forward until an unfortunate downward move:

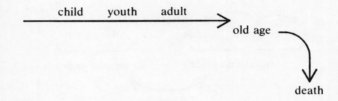

[1a]

An alternative image of human development would place childhood and youth in some degree of tension: Adulthood is then conceived as the continuing synthesis of childlike attitudes and the critical faculties of youth.

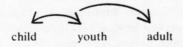

[1b]

Although this diagram is an improvement over the first, it is still incomplete. The questions of old age and death do not appear at all. The "fourth stage" which Dunne speaks of does not fit into this scheme. What was called a "second childhood" has to be added, but this addition changes the other three:

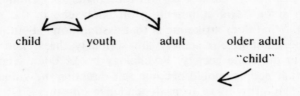

[1c]

If we go one step further in recognizing the older adult, the diagram looks this way:

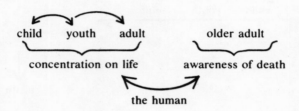

[1d]

In this final picture one can see both the legitimacy and the inadequacy of identifying old age and childhood. Old age does have to recover the attitude of childhood, but it must also include the other stages of life. The old person never ceases to be adult even as he or she becomes childlike. Adulthood, I shall claim is inadequately conceived unless it includes the awareness of one's own personal weakness and imminent death. To accept human life is to accept its opposite, death. That is the paradox toward which humans move from the beginning. If adulthood is the ideal, then adulthood has to include this paradox.

I would like now to describe more systematically the four operative meanings of adult in contemporary English. They are:
1. Synonymous with pornographic
2. Chronological or biological point of development

3. Ideal of rational, factual, economically productive individual
4. Ideal of maturity, integrity of life and death

1. Pornographic

Many people might suppose that this first meaning can be dismissed as unimportant and accidental. However, as old age is an interpretive key from one side, pornography is an important phenomenon at the other end. One thing is certain: The use of the word "adult" to mean pornographic has grown rapidly. Of the four meanings this one has been the fastest growing in the 1960s and 1970s. Adult entertainment, adult movie, and adult bookstore need no explanation any more in nearly all parts of the country. The adult entertainment area is most evident in the center of cities, but the "adult industries" serve small-town, rural, and suburban populations.

One definition of pornography is the presentation of sex without some larger human context. The search for "artistic pornography" is almost a contradiction in terms because pornography lacks sufficient human material to be artistic. By the same definition, however, pornography is not a moral horror; it is merely an underdevelopment of artistic and moral sensitivity. Pornography in our culture has become closely allied with drug abuse, violence, and the degrading of women. Pornography under some kinds of control might not be so bad. Or stated differently: Trying to stamp out pornography may make no sense if pornography is deeply rooted in our culture. The absence of pornography in such a society may be worse than its presence. On the basis of my overall analysis of adulthood I will claim that pornography in some form or other is the counterimage to our dominant ideal of adulthood.

2. Chronological/Biological Point

This meaning of adult is the clearest of the four even though there is some ambiguity in the relation between calendar time and organismic time. Some people seem to grow up quickly, some people seem to age slowly; some people who are 65 look 45 and vice versa. Nonetheless, there are unavoidable realities to the aging process. Girls may develop faster than boys, but eventually the boys catch up. Despite the ability of some people "to keep their youth," everyone eventually ages and dies.

For my purposes here the variations in relating biological and chronological age are not important. What is clear is that society uses adult and child to characterize two stages of life. Children may argue about the age at which they cease to be children, but they don't challenge the existence of the two categories: adult and child. I have said that there have always been some variations as to the age when children become adults. Our era is probably more confused than the past because of the extended span of adolescence and youth. What everyone does seem to agree upon is that if you wait long enough you are bound to become an adult in the chronological/biological sense.

3. Rational, Objective, Productive Individual

I have already noted that this third meaning (and the fourth as well) overlaps the chronological/biological meaning. There is nonetheless an important difference between this third meaning which relies on psychosocial criteria and the second meaning which is measured by the calendar. The law may *presume* you are adult after a certain age, but it is quite conceivable that a 30- or 40-year-old has never grown up in a psychological and social sense.

What is the chief mark of having become adult in one's life? Our society looks to reason as a psychological characteristic and ability to work as a social criterion. The two regularly go together. If one is not a reasonable being, one probably cannot hold a job. The child's tutelage is a progress toward the use of the mind in a world that exists objectively outside the mind. The child is thought to be immersed in subjective feelings which obstruct his or her ability to see the world as it is.

A chief mark of the childish is dependence. One is not fully a human being while one is dependent upon adults for all forms of sustenance. The human offspring from before birth is totally dependent upon the mother for nourishment. During infancy the child needs constant physical and psychic help from adults. As for being economically productive, the child remains for many years almost completely helpless. Becoming adult is conceived of as ending this radical dependence. The person acquires the ability to think, to organize, to judge, and to work.

At the center of this description is the word "reason" or "rational." Rationality and adulthood become almost synonymous. Where did such a view come from? Roger Gould writes that "the preferred view that adults are rational is a strongly held prejudice of mankind and has fit well the needs of a Christian theology and a structure of civilization built on the law."[9] The reference to theology here in addition to law may be surprising, but there is some basis to tracing concern for reason to Christian and Greco-Roman ideas. In an article entitled "Christian Adulthood" William Bouwsma makes a contrast similar to the one I am making between two ideals of adulthood. The one which stresses rational individuals he calls "historic Christianity" which he seems to see as a corruption of a biblical meaning of adulthood.[10]

Criticism of Hellenic or Christian emphasis on reason has to take account of a narrowing in the meaning of reason during recent centuries. The past shouldn't be attacked on the basis of the present meaning of terms. In the case of reason, we now have both a narrower and a more powerful meaning of the word. It is that meaning which has to be questioned when offered as the ideal for individuals and societies.

The movement called "Enlightenment" was the attempt to free reason from the shackles of any authority. "Dare to be wise—think for oneself"[11] was the central motto of the Enlightenment. In the view of eighteenth- and nineteenth-century *illuminati* the world was becoming adult and the countries of the Western Enlightenment were leading the way. Individuals could participate in this forward movement to the extent that they could use their minds to abstract, to objectify, and to master the environment.

The individual was the central concern of this progress, that is, the individual and his or her reason. Each individual's progress in this forward movement could be measured. Louis Terman, one of the fathers of the IQ test, wrote that "an individual is intelligent in proportion as he is able to carry on abstract thinking."[12] I would not be doing violence to that quotation if I replaced the word "intelligent" with adult. No higher ideal was posited than intelligence—meaning the ability to think abstractly. This ability, it was believed, could be directly correlated with people's acquisition of wealth, virtue, and happiness.

The IQ mentality has been vigorously attacked in recent times and the racial/nationalistic crudities associated with IQ tests have been curtailed. Still, the basis of criticism has not been entirely clear. The IQ maintains a significant hold on United States education because it does fit in with our ideal of intelligence. Much of the criticism has been directed merely toward correcting biases. Educational systems still try to measure intelligence more accurately so as to guide better the movement toward adulthood.

The ideal that is regularly assumed throughout our popular literature is independence of the individual. Bestselling books constantly work the theme of how to get control of your life. There is a struggle for power, it is presumed, and the choices are to manage or to be managed. The adult-minded person is to free himself from all domination including that of his own feelings. The adult is one who takes charge and sees clearly what his options are. With machinelike accuracy he makes the right decisions. He takes responsibility for the choices which determine his life.

As a clear example of this ideal consider the extraordinarily successful book *I'm OK–You're OK*.[13] Author Thomas Harris popularized a system of psychology called Transactional Analysis. His starting point is a model of the human person composed of three parts: parent, child, and adult. What is immediately striking is not the use of ordinary words and imagery in a scientific system. Freud after all tried to start his system with terms close to ordinary German speech.[14] Rather, it is the particular choice of imagery and language. Parent and adult are separated and both set in relation to child. Adult and child here are obviously not just chronological categories. Child in relation to both adult and parent has specific meanings tied to a psychosocial ideal.

The position of parent outside adult is the most intriguing part of the scheme. While it is obvious that not all adults are parents, it would seem that nearly all parents are adults. Of course, the actions of a parent may not always be adult (as distinct from the actions of *an* adult). But is it to be presumed that one can never act as parent and at the same time be adult?

The names in the model fairly well determine what can be said of each element. The parent cannot be adult because of his or her involvement with another person and especially because that other person does not act from reason and objectivity. The adult part is able to remain above the fray and coolly calculate the proper way to act. The image which Harris can easily employ is the computer: "The adult is a data-processing computer which grinds out decisions after computing the information from 3 sources: the Parent, the Child, and the data which the Adult has gathered and is gathering."[15]

Consistent with the choice to set adult next to parent and child, the ideal of adulthood is identified with rational objectivity. Adulthood starts very early in life, but it is set along a narrow track. The "Adult's ability to find out for himself" is contrasted to the "taught concept of life in his Parent and the felt concept of life in his Child."[16]

The significance of *I'm OK – You're OK* is that it captures so well the dominant ideal of adulthood in our society. Like so many self-help manuals in the United States the big question is not where to go but how to get there. The ideal to be sought receives very little examination in this kind of literature. The individual, it is assumed, wants to be strong, healthy, liberated, and successful. To be an individual at all connotes those qualities of independence and self-determination. Everyone supposedly has the chance to be successful in this way. If there are people at the margins of society who do not seem to be successful, they simply have to try harder or receive help until they are ready to go it alone.

Old age, as I have already noted, is the most intractable

challenge to this ideal both because it is "incurable" and because it is where the self-possessed individuals eventually land. The only way to deal with the problem of old age here is to postpone it as long as possible and keep it out of sight. A society that is primarily concerned with rational and technical productivity does not know what to do about old age.

The identification of adulthood with the strong, rational, productive individual hits older men the hardest. White men in United States society do not on the average live much beyond "retirement age." They seem to sense the logic that if to be a man is to be a worker, then to retire is to cease to be a man. Extending the retirement age may help a little, but it is still following a policy of postponement. The underlying problem is the identification of human adulthood with rational and technical forms of productivity. If that ideal kills men after retirement, it may also be unhealthy before retirement. The case of women has been different; one cannot immediately say better or worse, just different. The history of women does not provide the perfect human ideal, but that history is one of the levers for questioning the ideal that has dominated men's lives in the United States.

4. Integration of Opposites, Maturity, Wholeness

The fourth meaning of adulthood, like the third, overlaps the chronological meaning of adult. That is, it forms part of the basis for society's designating the point when people become adults. It is an ideal which begins in infancy and can continue to grow throughout life. Whereas rationality is assumed to be firmly secured by people in their 20s or 30s, the ideal of maturity to be described now is both slower in coming and never completely secured in life.

As with the third meaning, one could also ask here: Where did the ideal come from? Befitting its paradoxical character, this ideal comes from contrasting sources: modern science and primitive wisdom, Eastern and Western religions, the experience of the healthiest people and the history of oppressed people. Christian writers who claim to discover this ideal in the Bible as the "true Christianity" have some basis. But Christian claims today need a dialogical context of Jewish and Eastern religion, ancient cultures and modern society. I would not wish to claim that this ideal is derived from Christian documents, but I think it is possible to claim that this ideal is compatible with much of the original and continuing impulse of the Christian movement.

This meaning of adulthood is marked by the synthesizing of what are often thought to be opposites. Psychologist George Lapassade has said that adulthood is a stage in which pleasure and pain are no longer separable.[17] Throughout much of life there may be a search for pleasure and a hope to avoid pain. The hope is always unrealistic and old age, if nothing before, proves that to be the case. At some age in life, if people are to experience the full range of humanity, they have to give up searching for the perfect pleasure. They need to discover that love for one's equal, care for those in need, and passion for justice involve a pleasure that also hurts. Pleasure and pain here are signposts for the union of opposites that is adulthood. The following three examples of union are especially noteworthy:

A. *Rational/Nonrational*

The third meaning of adult holds out the rational individual as the highest ideal. While not repudiating rationality, this fourth meaning of adult puts reason at the service of life. That means the admission of the nonrational as a positive force. Whereas the word "irrational" connotes violence and the destruction of the rational, the word "nonrational" simply refers to what is not rational and to all that reason abstracts from. Adult behavior would then mean that sometimes a person acts reasonably and sometimes he or she doesn't. Behavior that is nonrational is not necessarily beyond all human control. The individual can let go of the self into a relational control which may include one's own feelings, other people, and the non-human environment. A parent playing a game with a small child does not always act rationally, but the behavior is appropriate—and adult.

Adult activity does not require the individual always to be

conscious and self-reflective. The person moves between poles of conscious self-direction and spontaneous reaction. In the image Martin Buber uses, "consciousness ought to play first violin but not be conductor."[18] Nothing is higher than reason, but something is broader, namely, the life of the organism in its environment. The adult person is able to control environmental factors when such control is appropriate. At other times the person can be quietly receptive to the human and non-human environment.

Toward one's own body the attitude is also one of conscious and reflective control at times. But even for the sake of that control the proper attitude is sometimes one of inattention. As John Dewey said, one's golf swing is not improved by always thinking of one's swing.[19] The same is true of innumerable other human gestures in which the body has been trained "to do its own thinking" and rational consciousness keeps quiet. From the first complex act of sucking a nipple to the last moment of giving up the spirit, the ideal of reason is not an adequate guide.

B. Dependence/Independence

The relation of dependence and independence is another expression of the union of opposites. In our society dependence/independence is of special importance for understanding the ideal of adulthood. Quite regularly, the movement toward adult is described as an increase of independence and a decrease of dependence. However, dependence vs. independence is not an accurate description of human choice. There are several forms of dependence and several forms of independence. While some forms of dependence are to be outgrown (e.g., economic dependence on parents), other relations that can be called dependent may be desirable (e.g., love for one's parents). While independence of some things may be worth striving for, independence as the final ideal of life is illusory and self-destructive.

No single word can capture the paradox of uniting independence and dependence. However, the word "interdependence" has become a helpful word. It has gained some currency especially in reference to international affairs. Even the most powerful country in the world is ineluctably related to the rest of the world in financial and ecological interdependence. The word could also be helpful in describing individual human beings. People are interdependent, that is, there is a necessary and desirable dependence of humans on one another. That interdependence can also be called "mutuality," a reciprocal giving and receiving in which everyone profits. If I depend on you and you depend on me, then there is a growing I, a growing you, and a growing we. With some change in the kind or degree of mutuality, the same principle is true of the non-human environment. We and the trees, we and the rivers, we and the minerals, constitute an interdependent world.

The paradox here is that one finds a strength in shedding the belief that one can be a masterful power. The discovery of an adult self is an acceptance of oneself as "one among many." The others always remain some threat to one's existence, but they also provide support. One doesn't always have to be struggling and striving. If one lets go, the world neither disappears from sight nor engulfs one's selfhood. Adulthood is that specific form of dependence (or interdependence) in which the illusion of self-sufficiency is recognized and one gratefully responds to the pain/pleasure of life.

C. *Life/Death*

The unavoidable puncturing of human independence is death. The choice here is between death as a cruel destroyer at the end of life and death as a factor throughout life which makes us receptive, gentle, and filled with care. The third meaning of adult can make little sense of death and relegates it to the end of life. This fourth meaning of adulthood incorporates death into all of life's activities. Small children have a strong sense of death (e.g., as reflected in fairy tales). As people grow up, death recedes to the background, but it should not be totally blocked from our awareness. As one becomes more adult, death begins to shade all our hopes, projects, and concerns.

Death raises the question of whether other humans and non-humans are opponents to be mastered or colleagues to be befriended. If rationality/objectivity is the ideal of adulthood, then the ideal is to master the world. But the ideal is shattered by death which seems to prove that life is a cruel hoax. If care and love is the ideal of adulthood, then one is called to befriend the world.

Death in this context is a severe test of our gestures of love, but death does not prove them useless. Younger people assume that death is the big worry of old age, but those who have lived by befriending life have often by old age befriended death as well.[20]

This fourth meaning of adulthood is one that is attainable only by exchanges between human groupings and between humans and non-humans. In reference to human groupings I would especially stress exchange across generational lines and sexual lines.

The third meaning of adulthood did not entirely exclude children. Nonetheless, a strong contrast is drawn between the small amount of a child's independence compared to the high degree of adult independence. Rationality and objectivity are conceived to be a progression away from the status of childhood. In the fourth meaning of adulthood, not only are children not excluded, but their presence and qualities are a key test of adulthood. To become adult is to recapture some of the qualities of childhood. The very young and the very old have much in common. Each helps to bring out qualities present but hidden in the other. Adulthood in this meaning can be evaluated only by an intergenerational community. If the generations were entirely segregated, then no one would be adult and no one would know what it means to be adult. We are not in that frightful situation, but modern society erects barriers between generations.

What is true of the intergenerational mix is also true of sexual diversity. The third meaning of adulthood has been described, as it is regularly and appropriately described, with the masculine pronoun. The ideal is the "individual and his reason." The fourth meaning of adulthood cannot be described without advertence to a pluralism that includes sexual elements. The ideal is a union of men, women, children, and others in which unity and differences grow together.

Especially in the nineteenth century, women were not thought to be rational, objective, and productive. To be a man was to have work that was recognized as economically productive. Women were in another realm needing for identity not work but a relation to "man's world." Women were spared the crisis of retirement in old age, but they had to face the question very early in life. In recent decades great numbers of women have entered the sector defined as work. What remains to be seen is whether women will change work or work will change women. That is, the fourth meaning of adulthood requires that work be placed at the service of a wider ideal of life and death. That ideal has been preserved in part within the sphere assigned to women. The question now is whether that meaning will get lost or whether a fuller meaning of adulthood will become available by reason of men and women learning from each other.

One final point remains in the interrelation of these four meanings. If the fourth is a fuller meaning than the third, where is the missing element of number three existing now? I said above that it may exist in healthy or distorted form in the "woman's sphere." But where does it exist for men? The answer, I suggest, is found in my first meaning of adult, that is, the pornographic. I said that this use of adult is not a bizarre accident. Pornography as an irrational concern with sex (and violence) is the underside of the ideal of adulthood represented by meaning number three.

Since human life is as a matter of fact not entirely rational and objective, then the rest of life has to show up somewhere. If rationality, independence, and objectivity are presented as the ultimate ideal, then the other side to life will come out in distorted and obsessive ways. There will be a disjunction of public and private persons, a separation of sex and care, and an addictive dependence on pleasures that cause guilty feelings. The actual operation of the pornography business supports this theory. The market of the pornographic trade is mostly male, white, middle-aged, married, respectable and wealthy. The same people who are thought to have the ideal of number three are the people who show up in number one.

A further confirmation of this thesis is a frightening one. I said that: *a*) the ideal of number three is constantly contrasted to children; *b*) the other side of number three is the pornographic. It would follow that the ultimate counterpoint to the ideal of adulthood in number three would be child pornography. It is impossible to find anyone in the United States who will defend child pornography and yet it is a multibillion-dollar industry. This fact can only mean that the practice goes to the core of our society's ideals and institutions. Child pornography suddenly attracted attention in 1977, but it has long been the underside of our society. This form of pornography has less to do with sex than with power though the two are intimately related. In a world where "self-determination" is the great ideal and yet most men feel powerless, the sexual domination of children is one sure release.[21]

Finally, in looking ahead to the next chapter it is already possible to see two educational ideals that correspond to the third and fourth meanings of adulthood. Ideals of adulthood can be correlated to educational systems. Which comes first is a chicken-or-egg question. The ideal is embodied in the pattern of education while that education continually reinforces the ideal. The link between ideal and institution is found in language and imagery.

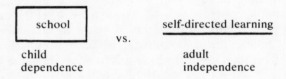

[2A]

In this model the governing ideal is the third meaning of adulthood: the rational and independent individual. Institutions are conceived to be restrictions on individual liberty. The adult learner is in charge of his own learning and learns only what interests him. The child, on the other hand, has to learn discipline and disciplines. Liberal reforms of school are imagined to be those which increase permissiveness for the individual within school.

The purpose of education here may be put under the term "self-actualization." A standard and contemporary definition would be that of Robert Blakely in the *Handbook of Adult Education*: "The purpose of American life and American education is, in this light, seen to be the development of individuals who will fulfill themselves and freely serve the society which values individuals."[22] First the individual is perfected and then society is served. A peculiarity of this definition is the fact that the individual is to serve the "society which values individuals." What if society doesn't value individuals? Apparently the stipulation that this is an "American" education takes care of that point since perhaps by definition American society values individuals.

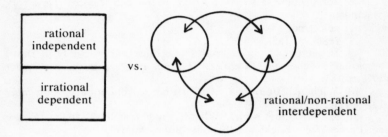

In the fourth meaning of adulthood the choice is not between school and self-directed learning or between child and adult. The choice is between authoritarian forms of organization that segregate by age, sex, or other categories and a community-based education in which people grow in interdependence. The purpose of education includes individual development, but the individual is situated in the realistic context of his or her environment. Kenneth Benne captures most of this meaning: "Educators must concern themselves with the individual's quest for identity, the quest for community, the proper uses of fraternity, the assumptions which underlie problems created by bureaucratic behavior, and the reeducation of persons in human relations."[23]

To describe an educational model for this ideal of adulthood it is not enough to describe a model of "adult education." We need a model of education that in being adequate for adults is at the same time inclusive of children. The test of any educational model is whether it helps adults and children move together toward an adulthood that is mature, wise, and integral. The details of that model are what we turn to in the next chapter.

Notes

1. Joseph Goldstein, "On Being Adult and Being an Adult in Secular Law," *Daedalus*, 105(Fall, 1976), p. 69.

2. Winthrop Jordan, "Searching for Adulthood in America," *Daedalus*, 105(Fall, 1976), p. 3.

3. *Ibid.*, p. 8.

4. *Ibid.*, p. 10.

5. See *Rite of Christian Initiation of Adults* (Washington, U.S. Catholic Conference, 1974).

6. John Dunne, *A Search for God in Time and Memory* (New York, Macmillan, 1969).

7. *Ibid.*, pp. 154–55.

8. *Ibid.*, p. 155.

9. Roger Gould, "The Phases of Adult Life: A Study in Developmental Psychology," *American Journal of Psychiatry*, November, 1972, p. 52.

10. William Bouwsma, "Christian Adulthood," *Daedalus*, 105(Spring, 1976), p. 77.

11. See Immanuel Kant, "What Is Enlightenment?" in *On History,* ed. Lewis White Beck (Indianapolis, Bobbs-Merrill, 1963).

12. See Benjamin Fine, *The Stranglehold of the IQ* (Garden City, Doubleday, 1975), p. 10.

13. Thomas Harris, *I'm OK–You're OK* (New York, Avon, 1973).

14. See Sigmund Freud, *The Question of Lay Analysis* (New York, W. W. Norton, 1959).

15. Harris, *op. cit.*, p. 53.

16. *Ibid.*, p. 51.

17. See Richard Sennett, *The Uses of Disorder* (New York, Knopf, 1970), p. 150.

18. Martin Buber, *Eclipse of God* (New York, Harper Torchbook, 1952), p. 39.

19. John Dewey, *Art as Experience* (New York, Capricorn, 1958), p. 109.

20. See Alan Knox, *Adult Development and Learning* (San Francisco, Jossey-Bass, 1977), p. 51.

21. See Gloria Steinem, "Pornography—Not Sex but the Obscene Use of Power," and Helen Dudar, "America Discovers Child Pornography," *Ms.*, August, 1977, pp. 43ff.

22. Quoted in Malcolm Knowles, ed., *Handbook of Adult Education in the United States* (Chicago, Adult Education Association, 1960), p. 6.

23. Kenneth Benne, *Education for Tragedy* (Lexington, University of Kentucky, 1967), p. 198.

3. An Educational Model

My intention in this chapter is to work out in more detail the way education would look if the fourth meaning of adulthood were the guide. As in the rest of this book, I am not proposing to bring into existence something completely new. The main problem is to find a more adequate language to describe what already exists. An inadequate language blocks our vision of what is now happening. Nietzsche's definition of creativity was the ability to name what is in full sight of everyone but is invisible because it has not yet been named.[1]

The naming of what already exists also enhances its effectiveness. A *system* of education needs names and descriptions so that each of the elements can play an effective role within an overall educational pattern. My description is of *one* educational model. The word "model" implies that there are other possibilities. A model is not right or wrong; rather it is more or less adequate. The relevant question for a model is whether it is both comprehensive and consistent; that is, does it cover all the obvious data (and possibly reveal more data) while retaining an inner logic to its imagery and language?

Before describing my model for the fourth meaning of adulthood, I would like to comment on existing educational language which reflects the third meaning of adulthood. When adulthood is conceived of in rationalistic and individualistic terms, there is really not an educational model at all. There is simply school as *the* form for educating people when they are children and amorphousness when education is referred to adult life.

37

At the center of this problem is the peculiar phrase "formal education." "Education" is a word that surely connotes form. It would seem, therefore, that "formal education" is a redundancy and that "non-formal education" is nearly a contradiction in terms. Why then is the phrase "formal education" used so frequently and what does it really mean?

I think that the answer is not difficult to find. When the identification of school and education was criticized, a distinction was introduced between "formal education" and the rest of education.

Most of the time "formal education" is simply a synonym for school. Those who wish to continue speaking as if school were practically coextensive with education can do so while occasionally interjecting the word "formal" before education. Those who are critical of the school's hegemony feel that they have opened the discussion to other possibilities. But have they? School— with all of its former connotations—controls the word "formal," which is of the essence of education. Money, people, power, and effort are never directed to what is without form. "Adult education" writers don't seem to notice that they paint themselves into a corner by saying: "The growing criticism of *formal education* for its continuing failures to provide more relevant education should also be applied to *adult education*."[2] Adult here can only mean not formal.

The constant, unexamined use of the phrase "formal education" is unhealthy both for school and for other forms of education. The phrase implies that school is a single, unchanging form. A re-form of school is impossible unless one speaks of variations in the form of school and subsidiary forms within the school (e.g., learning centers in addition to classrooms). Even worse is the position of non-school forms of education which are necessarily nameless. Obviously, everyone acknowledges "random experiential learning," but what can be said of it except that it happens?[3]

One of the reforms needed in schools is to break their exclusive identification with children. If formal education equals school and school equals children, the education of adults is left formless and nameless. The worldwide adult education movement flounders on this point. UNESCO has an "out-of-school committee," which tells us only something negative. John Lowe puzzles over the fact that "the very idea of *post-school* education still seems paradoxical to many policy-makers and teachers."[4] Out-of-school and post-school will never define educational tasks and policies.

"Formal" and "informal" are adjectives that are widely used. I would grant that one can sensibly speak about formal and informal learning. An organism can learn without any attention to form. One might even learn something while unconscious. Certainly there is learning that occurs when there is no intention to learn on the part of the learner. Our environment teaches us far more than we are ever consciously aware of. If one were to extend the word "form" to all organization of experience, then in strictest logic no learning is informal or nonformal or formless. However, the forms which are referred to here are simply present with learning rather than established for learning.

"Education" is a word that connotes more form and organization than does the word "learning." Even here if someone wishes to describe a set of experiences as "informal education," one cannot say that this is an abuse of language. But if informal education is always set against a narrow and monolithic meaning of "formal education," then the significance of this language has to be challenged. With the phrase "informal school" I think we indeed come to a contradiction in terms. "School" is a word with a high degree of formality. "Formal schooling" is a redundancy and "informal school" is a bad name for attempted school reform.

Much of the great uprising in the 1960s was directed at school, as if liberation from school were the means to freedom. The critics of the school were often unclear as to what was wrong with school and what was to be the educational alternative. Change within school usually went in the direction of letting each child "do his own thing."[5] The greater revolution seemed to be to take down the school walls and let life do the educating. But the problem of form quickly resurfaces and if the word "formal" has been given over to current school form, how can any group begin to address the problem?

Educational reforms, both in recent and in distant United

States history, have been afflicted with a strange unrealism. There has been a search for the perfect school that would have none of the limitations that the word "form" includes, in short, a "nonschool school."[6] Utopian expectations from the school are regularly disappointed. Those who have some luxury in society can afford to be severely critical of schools. Poor people get frustrated by the performance of schools, but no one ever hears them demanding liberation from school. Thomas Cottle, a sensitive conversationalist with the poor, writes: "To say that our public schools need restructuring is an understatement. But to say that, given their shabby state, it may be better for children to be out of school is nonsense, the idle speculation of people who have never met excluded children, never heard their stories."[7]

In this section I would like to describe a movement, especially among historians, to name other forms of education besides school. I think that this movement is a good one even though it has to go farther. The historical materials should be helpful in thinking through a model for the twentieth century.

What other social forms carry out something definite enough to be called "education" but distinct from the form called "school"? A common answer given by historical-minded writers is "family and church." Contemporary writers regularly note other influences, for example, television. Still, a common way to refer to the diversity of educational forms in United States life is to cite the triad of family-church-school.

John Dewey early in this century wrote of the family and church as educational possibilities. However, he usually turns quickly to the school as the only agency that can bear the burden of education. Lawrence Cremin says that Dewey committed the "genetic fallacy" by assuming that because family and church did not originate from an educational intention, they cannot provide an educational function.[8] Perhaps Cremin is right, but it seems to me that Dewey was concerned not merely with the origin of family and church but with their state of health in the twentieth century. He saw the family as incapable of providing the training it once did; he also saw the Christian church as having lost its control of religious life.[9]

Having assumed the triad of family-church-school, Dewey's

criticism of family and church tends to reinforce the school's hegemony. Schools which in the nineteenth century had been expected to do much were now expected to do more. Histories of education continued to be almost entirely histories of school. Departments of education and teacher-training schools gave the impression that to study education was to prepare for work in schools.

An important shift in the historiography of education occurred with Bernard Bailyn's *Education in the Forming of American Society* (1960).[10] Bailyn seriously pursued the distinction which had too quickly been dismissed by others. Family and church were found to be important forms of education in the colonial period. At that time school was but a minor part of the story. Only in the nineteenth century did schools gain control of the story. Lawrence Cremin in his historical writing of the 1960s and 1970s adopted a framework similar to Bailyn's. He has consistently resisted equating the history of education and the history of schools.[11]

Family-church-school together with some other forms (e.g., apprenticeship) give us a good picture of the seventeenth-century colonies. The twentieth century is neither a replica of the seventeenth century nor a completely new picture; it is a picture constantly retouched and gradually taking new shape. The terms "family-church-school" cannot bear the major burden of a twentieth-century model of education.

Dewey was correct in perceiving a change in the family's position in the nineteenth century. But contrary to what might have been expected then, the family did not decline in importance. As some functions left the family, its primary effect became more important. To understand the family today one must place it in a context of non-familial social forms different from either the seventeenth or the nineteenth centuries. "Church" is also inadequate for describing the other main form of education. Christian churches remain today as some of the religious institutions in society. They do not have the direct and visible power they once had. Similar to the family, the church in proper context might offer several contributions to education in the twentieth century.

Continuity and differences regarding school-family-church

should be noted. The colonialists were strong believers in school especially because of the need to read the Scriptures and the doctrines of the Puritan church. In 1647 the General Court of Massachusetts encouraged every township of fifty householders to hire a teacher. Reading schools would counter "one chief project of that old deluder Satan, to keep men from knowledge of the Scriptures."[12] Schools in fact had already sprung up in the decade preceding this law. Although Massachusetts remained the leader in its concern with schools and literacy, schools were also begun in Virginia and the other colonies.

Family life in the colonies was both regular and comprehensive. That is, there was a definite pattern of organization and authority with little room for variety. The family was the model of government and also the basis for God's contact with people. Besides a tightly consistent pattern, the family's role encompassed more than it does today. Most of what was work took place in the setting of the home and in proximity to the family. Agriculture was a family affair and manufacturing of products was for the most part done in the home. When a boy was apprenticed, therefore, it was not only the learning of a new trade but entrance to a new family.[13]

The church in the seventeenth century was also a dominant institution. The ideal of a theocracy was brought from Europe to many of the colonies. A Christian commonwealth was envisioned, but it never really worked out. The church is a voluntary organization in a way the family can never be; that fact conditions everything that the church can do educationally.

It is a long-standing tradition to appeal to "the church" for "morality" while society goes about its main business without much advertence to actual churches. Already by 1649 in Boston the case was: "Pastor and teacher pleaded for morality from the pulpit and catechized the children of the church in Sabbath classes; yet education was basically a civil affair, and morality was defined in law and enforced in the courts."[14] I think that this three-century tradition needs careful examination in church circles. To say that education is a school-family-church affair may sound like a vote of confidence in churches. However, the implication may be that the church is supposed to inculcate morals or offer adult education. Accepting that role may prevent churches from having a significant role in education through sponsoring schools, affecting family life, influencing the work sector, and providing retreats.

If family-church-school is not an adequate model for twentieth-century adulthood, what is the alternative? I would now like to offer an institutional model that would support the fourth meaning of adulthood, that is, an integrity born from the synthesis of opposites. The model would have this shape:

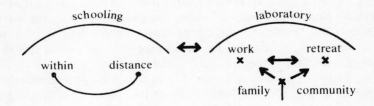

General Comments

The first distinction of form is between schooling and what I call "laboratory." I am not entirely satisfied with the second name, but the distinction is a clear one, especially today. There is a distinct form for schooling which needs acknowledgment and perhaps defense. As a complement to schooling there is another kind of learning that is much more physical and experimental. We learn by doing certain things in life, making mistakes, and acquiring "know-how." Much of what we know in this way is not even conscious.

The threefold division within the laboratory form highlights elements that are present in everyone's life. A problem in contemporary society is that these three do exist but mainly in segregation by age. Family is assumed to provide children with "preschool" education or socialization, work is what adults do after school, and retreat is what the old are assigned to when they retire from work. The model proposed here would break through the segregation by age. Everybody at any age needs the support of family/community, everyone needs work, and everyone needs some retreat. And all of us need institutional forms which make those educational possibilities available to us.[15]

A. Schooling

A first distinction to note here is one between school and schooling. *School* refers to the institution and the building while *schooling* is a form of learning. Within a school more things than schooling do occur and should occur. In addition, there are many ways to organize a school. An important movement at present is to have many small schools inside of large schools.[16] By the word "schooling" I refer to something narrower and less flexible in meaning. Schooling is a mode of learning that connotes a specific set of materials, intentions, and results.

Before describing schooling I have to admit its close relationship to school and the limitations of that word. "School" is a word that has been intimately related to childhood and youth. Part of my concern, of course, is to move toward a meaning of school and schooling that would include adult activity. The resistance to that idea is often buried deep in the psyche of grownups. Apparently it is a common experience for grownups to have a recurrent nightmare in which they are back in school as children and failing in their studies.[17] Why fight for a word with such bad connotations? The reasons are twofold: 1) "Schooling" is the proper and ancient term for a form of learning that is more indispensable than ever for everyone; 2) Good schools already involve in their operations many adults in many ways.

Schooling refers to a form in which people intentionally use space, time, materials, and people to acquire knowledge and skills. The school's center is the tool of literacy which allows the learner to contact not only the living but the dead.[18] The *space* for schooling is usually a school, but it can be any physical place whose primary use is directed to learning. The *time* involved is an extensive part of a day or week and the commitment extends for years. Each learner need not stay for several years, but schooling as a form requires continuity over a long period. The *materials* of schooling are books and related artifacts. Each school need not have a library, but schooling involves the use of library materials. The *persons* of schooling are a faculty who have the background, time, and ability to help the learners in their efforts.

This description of schooling does not assume that the learners are children. Very young children are not ready for school though an infant might profit from small amounts of schooling. From the first days of life a parent begins conveying to the child the elements of literacy.[19] Schooling can begin almost at birth and can continue almost to death.

We refer to certain people as being of "school age," about 6 years to 18 years old. This identification of school and children is not healthy for either child or adult. Schooling ought to be for everyone some of the time and for no one all of the time. Student and child ought to be distinguished in meaning even in those schools where all the students happen to be children.

Schools already involve adults, at least those adults who are teachers, administrators, coaches, and custodians. School also involves adults from a broader community, at least the parents of children. A hopeful sign today is that in some schools more adults are being involved and in more ways. At a national level a helpful step would be an "educational bill of rights"[20] that guarantees sixteen years of free schooling to be spread in one's life as desired. At local levels, the first step is to change laws that discourage adult participation in schooling. Some states actually have laws that forbid schools to be used for the education of adults.

Universities are the obvious places for adults who wish schooling. Universities have begun moving out to a broader adult population and the community college has been more willing to take on the task, but sometimes hasn't the resources to handle it. Universities and colleges have a distance to go before adults of any age will feel comfortable in the setting.

Elementary schools, interestingly enough, are often more effective in crossing generational lines. The elementary school in the United States has traditionally been "community" based. Over the past century the control of schools has shifted from the local base to distant school boards. Nonetheless, some power and flexibility remain in each school for devising new means of adult participation. For example, a school might have a program in which a parent replaces for a day his or her child. Some schools involve parents in a multiplicity of auxiliary jobs. A school counsellor today may best operate by bringing in people from dozens of professions.

The non-public school often has the liberty to experiment here beyond what the public school can try. One might even say that private and church-related schools have a duty to experiment in involving adults. Also, schools in urban ghettoes are sometimes forced to be imaginative in their relations to parents, neighborhoods, and business people. Schools with poor buildings and underpaid staffs can improve their lot and contribute to United States education if they make intergenerational exchange their vocation.

B. Schooling: Distance/Within

I wish to examine in this section a different aspect of schooling. In the diagram of the model there is a continuous line between "within" and "distance." Schooling is of its nature a distancing of oneself from the personal involvements of love and work. Schooling is a dispassionate examination of what the best minds of the human race have to say. Access to books and theoretical learning is among the most powerful forces in the world. But precisely because schooling is open and free inquiry, it threatens to overwhelm the mind with limitless possibility.

In practice no one starts to learn except from within existing premises, biases, and interests. Materials have to be selected from an almost infinite range of possibilities. The learner brings to schooling his or her experience, whatever it may be. Schooling has to begin from within some personally experienced world. At the same time this form of learning is intended to bring some longer-ranged or wider-angled perspective to the assumed premises and personal data. In this sense schooling "ob-jectifies," that is, we attempt to get a question or situation in front of us for careful examination. "Objective" has another meaning, viz., the absence of a personal subject, working presuppositions, and passionate interest. In that sense of the term, objective schooling is neither possible nor desirable.

My use of "within" and "distance" is an attempt to get at this complex issue. These two words express what is always a psychological tension in schooling. In contrast, the words "subjective" and "objective" fail to clarify the human dilemma. On any human issue the choice for a human being is not to be inside or outside the issue. The question is how to relate one's experience from within and one's capacity as a thinker to distance oneself. Schooling is a moment for the emphasis of distancing though never to the complete exclusions of experience from within.

The greater the human involvement, the greater is the tension between these moments. As one passes from mathematics to biology to social studies the tension increases. The problem is especially acute in areas of morality and religion. If one approaches mathematics with the categories of objective and subjective, no problem develops. Everyone knows that objective answers count and subjective answers are irrelevant. However, objective and subjective applied to religion do violence to the material. Either religion gets eliminated from school because it is not objective enough or else religion is reduced to a collection of strange objects and subjective phantasies. Morality undergoes a similar fate. It shows up in the form of legalism on one side and a subjective search for "values" on the other.

The framework proposed here might be called "intersubjective," an exchange between persons that includes moments of objectifying or distancing.[21] Religion would be taught, learned, and studied by groups of people who appreciate their own religious lives and compare their positions to other groups. That would be an *adult understanding* of religion. One does not step outside of religious presuppositions to see the "objective" truth. Personal involvement in living religiously is not assumed to be an obstacle to understanding religion. Any tendency toward *subjectivism* in religion is best corrected by intersubjective understanding. For example, while teaching a course on "Christian Morality" I have used as an assigned topic: Jewish reaction to Christian interpretation of Jewish morality. The students learn about *both* Judaism *and* Christianity. They also learn that another group's perspective can be a help to appreciating one's own religion and a correcting of one's own biases.

The working out of the tension of within/distance varies

with age, background, and interests. A small child may profit from immersion in a religious group's practices. A young adult may need and wish a strong dose of critical analysis. If everyone in a class is, for example, Jewish, then one can make assumptions that are not possible if a class is religiously varied. There is nothing academically illegitimate about teaching almost exclusively Jewish (Catholic, Moslem, Lutheran, etc.) concerns in a specific class, course, or curriculum. Academic legitimacy depends on a larger context which should offer some choice of material and diversity of interpretations. Diversity should extend, at least at times, to a mixture of religions in a class. Whether or not that happens to be the case, a cardinal test of any study is whether disparaging remarks are made about other groups. Absence of Jews in a class is no excuse for comparisons in which Jews always come out the losers.

Teachers have to distance themselves from their religious convictions in the act of teaching. However, teachers aren't always engaged in teaching. A teacher's own religious life need not be flaunted all the time but neither should it have to be hidden.[22] The teacher's religion is simply part of the rich store that he or she brings to teaching. We would generally assume that a critical-minded Catholic is best prepared to teach Catholicism while a prepared Jew would teach Judaism. But it is not inconceivable that a Jew might teach Catholicism to Catholics. As a start, any cooperation across religious lines might improve teaching for everyone.

While some emphases vary according to context, what I am describing as schooling in religion is not essentially different for public and non-public schools. An academically respectable course in a church-supported school should be legally and academically acceptable in a public school. There is no inherent reason why a Catholic teacher cannot teach a course on sacraments in a public school. This principle does not remove all reasons for a church sponsoring its own schools. Neither does it solve the conflicts about introducing religion into the curriculum of the public school. The presence of more adults here would be a help. Otherwise, there is the suspicion that teachers may be taking children away from the religion of their parents. Schooling is seldom that effective anyway and is only a small part of education. Religious education is not equivalent to schooling in religion, but an intelligent examination of religion in school would be a help to everyone.

C. *Laboratory: Family/Community*

The laboratory or non-schooling part of education includes three elements: family/community, work, and retreat. The first element, *family/community*, is so important that I will devote all of Chapter Five to it. The first experience which practically all children have is with the family. It is a powerful form of education.

There is no evidence that the family is about to go out of existence or that it will be less important in the future. However, I will describe several crucial changes. First, there is a continuous change in the family's context which calls for special attention today. A second change is the human race's gradually coming to control procreation. A third is the fact of fewer adults living in family units. Fewer adults in family units need not be bad either for the family or for those adults, but this change is a precarious shift for the human race. My reference is always to family/community rather than to family so that there will be room to explore these changes. We will discuss this issue further in Chapter Five.

D. *Laboratory: Work*

The average person in the twentieth-century United States spends only half as much time "at work" as a person in the nineteenth century. Nonetheless, work is still important to anyone's sense of worth and identity. Work itself educates and education may also be directed toward the training for work. For the contemporary adult, work issues may be the most likely point of entry for interest in education. A man who is unemployed will be interested in any education that promises a job. A woman whose main work has been "housewife" may be looking for a way to shift her work role. Rapid changes in the technological areas make continuing education a necessity for workers. The

Johnstone study found that fully one-third of "adult education" offerings were related to job training.

The principle that was stated for school also applies to work: Work should be for everyone some of the time and for no one all of the time. As school was given over to children so work was also segregated. Work has been mainly the province of males between 16 and 65 years old. What children, women, and old people did was often not recognized as work. Eventually, what is not named "work" ceases to be humanly productive and becomes confining drudgery.

The main change needed with work is to change the relation of work and life. That means changing the interplay of school-family/community—work—retreat. Work ought to spill over in the direction of the young, the old, and women. At the same time other concerns would complement work in the lives of many men.

Children need something productive to do besides schooling. Nineteenth-century laws which protected children from labor exploitation can run counter to today's need. Children still need protection from exploitative employers, but they also need contact with the adult world and useful work.[23] In some primitive societies there is little separation of child's play and adult work. With early industrial society work became heavy, mechanical, and boring. But in our late industrial society much of the scientific work needs an element of play and much of the "service" part of the economy is better "played at" than labored. We need to rediscover the primitive relation of work and play which would also challenge our exclusion of children from work.[24]

For youth in school we need work/study programs. The planning of these programs is no easy task, but it is not impossible to arrange them. Innumerable jobs exist in the service area and such jobs go begging. The problem seems to be in developing an attitude whereby children would see the value to themselves and others in work. Adults would also have to have this attitude and make the necessary institutional arrangements.

Young people have already gone some distance in developing a work/study arrangement. The presumption that people go to school and then go to work is not accurate today. Three-fourths of college students work at other jobs. The average age of a community college student is about 27, indicative that he or she has probably been working already and quite likely is continuing to work while going to school. We are not faced with the problem of inventing a completely new relationship but of acknowledging what now exists and then making the relationship more effective as an educational experience.[25]

At the other end of the age spectrum there is a growing recognition of the questionable relation between work and life for the old. It makes little sense for people to work full time until some arbitrary line after which they are no longer workers. One should be able to retire from many jobs but never have to retire from work. Workers who are bored by what they do but have the security of waiting for retirement are not being served well nor are employers receiving a fair effort for a just wage.

Education has to be provided in conjunction with work so that workers can either do the job better or move to new work. The responsibility ought to be shared by the government and the employer. The government's role should be mainly one of providing tax credits or direct grants. The employer ought to provide on-the-job training or else the time, money, and motivation to get work-related education off the job. Corporations already engage in some of this activity but usually in narrow ways. While one cannot expect corporations to be entirely altruistic, they might be pushed beyond exclusively self-serving policies. Enlightened educational policy in countries like Sweden, Japan, and Yugoslavia threatens the power of the United States company.[26] For the long-range and broad health of the productive economy, employers should see that education and work are colleagues and not enemies.

E. Laboratory: Retreat

A funny thing happened to retreats as they were disappearing from the church; they were discovered by psychologists and educationalists.[27] Retreats didn't entirely disappear from churches, but they were thought by many people to be outdated. Or the traditional quiet retreat became a very talkative affair in

Catholic and Protestant churches. Over the last decade, however, a new awareness has been growing of the need for a contemplative or quiet zone in one's life. Retreat is a counterpoint to the rest of a person's education. If retreat becomes unhinged from a connection to public action, it can be unhealthy, but so can work without quiet reflection.

Retreat, like work and schooling, ought to be for everyone some of the time and for no one all of the time. Certain groups were assigned retreat as their station in life. These groups understandably are rebelling against their segregation. At the same time their forced possession of retreat may provide them with something to teach other groups. Old people have been placed in retreat or retirement because society did not understand either work or retreat. Now it is time for the old to teach retreat and retirement to everyone else.

Women, especially in the nineteenth century, were also given this part to play. "Woman's noblest station is retreat," Mary Tucker could say in 1802 at the beginning of the historical period that would enforce this ideal.[28] Work moved out of the home in the nineteenth century, but women did not. The home was a retreat from the evils of a newly urbanized world. The woman was to be the center and heart of the home. Women were allowed into teaching and nursing because these jobs were thought to be works of the heart and not of the head. The nineteenth century was not wrong in looking for retreats, but the design of home-mother-retreat over against factory-father-work was a bad division of labor. The burden became intolerable upon the mother. She had to raise the child *in retreat from* the city while preparing the child to live *within* the city.[29]

As with work there are two aspects of retreat education: Retreat is itself educational and there can also be education for retreat. The latter concern has been incorporated within United States education. In the Johnstone study, one-fifth of all offerings came under the broad category of "leisure concerns." Taking a course on how to use one's free time seems to make sense to many people. However, the bigger test of understanding is whether retreat itself can be seen as a necessary part of education.

Everyone does have some quiet in his or her life. To start

with the obvious, nearly a third of life is spent sleeping. Sleep is a gift to the humans which allows dreaming to occur and gives a sense of new starts. Even while awake everyone needs moments for dreaming and places where one can rest. The human organism needs the rhythm of going outward and returning to a center. Without that return to the self's center, the rest of education would be a jumble and not personally owned by the learner.

The need for institutionalizing retreat has probably become more acute in the contemporary world with its stream of noise. Churches in the past have been spaces of quiet and they could still offer that service. That's not the only service a church can supply, but retreat is certainly a value that is thoroughly consistent with the church's past. Other institutions should cooperate in this venture so that people can have quiet minutes each day and occasional days or weekends of retreat.

One of the chief concerns of the work site should be that it has space and time for quiet reflection. Here, too, it is ultimately to the employer's self-interest that the job be complemented by retreat. School buildings, besides containing schooling, should provide zones of retreat. Herbert Kohl notes: "Almost without exception the students want spaces that are private, in which they can be alone, or alone with a few friends, and talk and work and think."[30]

In our day we are encouraged to work with others, to "have relationships," and to do something productive. I wouldn't wish to speak against these things, but a key test of each of them is the presence of silence. A community is a group of people who provide a place of silence at the center. Can one be alone and not be lonely? Can one confront the solitude that is part of the human condition and not be destroyed by it? The existence of a retreat that is at the center of one's person and the center of a community is a supreme test of education.

Notes

1. See: Edmundo O'Gorman, *The Invention of America* (Bloomington, University of Indiana, 1961), p. 168.

2. Jack London, "Adult Education for the 1970's: Promise or Illusion?" *Adult Education,* 24(1973), p. 61.

3. See: Paul Bergevin, *A Philosophy for Adult Education* (New York, Seabury, 1967), pp. 52, 59.

4. Lowe, *op. cit.*, p. 27.

5. The interesting connection between sexism and the supposedly liberal school which allows each student to do "his own thing" is explored in Barbara Grizzuti Harrison, *Unlearning the Lie: Sexism in School* (New York, Liveright, 1973), especially p. 25.

6. See the criticism along these lines in Allen Graubard, *Free the Children* (New York, Pantheon, 1972).

7. Thomas Cottle, *Barred from School* (Washington, New Republic, 1976), p. 166.

8. Lawrence Cremin, *Public Education* (New York, Basic, 1976), p. 21.

9. In reference to the family, see John Dewey, *Dewey on Education,* ed. Martin Dworkin (New York, Teachers College, 1959); pp. 33-49. and in reference to the church, see John Dewey, *A Common Faith* (New Haven, Yale, 1960).

10. Bernard Bailyn, *Education in the Forming of American Society* (New York, Vintage, 1960).

11. See: Lawrence Cremin, *American Education: The Colonial Experience 1607–1783* (New York, Harper, 1970).

12. See: Edmund Morgan, *The Puritan Family* (New York, Harper Torchbook, 1966), p. 88.

13. See *Ibid.*, pp. 120ff.

14. Darrett Rutman, *Winthrop's Boston: Portrait of a Puritan Town 1630–1649* (Chapel Hill, University of North Carolina, 1965), p. 258.

15. On the segregation of these elements by age, see Wirtz, *op. cit.*

16. See James Coleman, *Youth* (Chicago, University of Chicago, 1974), pp. 154f.

17. See John Holt, *How Children Fail* (New York, Delta, 1964), pp. 63f.

18. See Hannah Arendt, *Between Past and Future* (New York, Viking, 1961), p. 195.

19. See Rudolph Schafer, *Mothering* (Cambridge, Harvard, 1977), pp. 73f.

20. See Theodore Hesburgh, *Patterns for Lifelong Learning* (San Francisco, Jossey-Bass, 1974), p. 15.

21. Philip Phenix, "Religion in Public Education: Principles and Issues," in *Religion in Public Education*, ed. David Engel (New York, Paulist, 1974), p. 67.

22. See Paul Goodman, "Reflections on Children's Rights," in *The Children's Rights Movement*, ed. Beatrice Gross and Ronald Gross (Garden City, Doubleday, 1977), p. 145.

23. See Coleman, *op. cit.*

24. See Joseph Chilton Pearce, *Magical Child* (New York, E. P. Dutton, 1977), pp. 199f: Erik Erikson, *Toys and Reason* (New York, Norton, 1977), p. 63.

25. See Wirtz, *op. cit.*, pp. 7, 28, 58.

26. See F. W. Jessup, *Lifelong Learning* (London, Pergamon, 1969), pp. 79ff; David Jenkins, *Job Power* (Baltimore, Penguin, 1974).

27. See Sidney Jourard, *Disclosing Man to Himself* (New York, Van Nostrand, 1968), p. 201; E. Fuller, Torrey, *The Death of Psychiatry* (New York, Penguin, 1975), pp. 165–67.

28. Quoted in Cott, *op. cit.*, p. 57.

29. See Kirk Jeffrey, "The Family as Utopian Retreat from the City: The Nineteenth Century Contribution," in *The Family, Communes and Utopian Society*, ed. Sallie Teselle (New York, Harper Torchbook, 1972).

30. Herbert Kohl, *On Teaching* (New York, Schocken, 1976), p. 115.

4. Religious Journey to Adulthood

In the second chapter we looked at two contrasting ideals of adulthood that are implicit in the culture. One ideal sees adulthood as the domain of strong, rational individuals. The other places reason at the service of life and death while the person works toward a reconciliation with the world. The third chapter showed the two directions which education takes according to the ideal of adulthood. In the first case education divides into "formal education" or school for children followed by self-directed learning for adults. In the second case education is an interplay of schooling—work—family/community—retreat across the generations.

In this chapter I wish to describe the religious correlation to this pattern of adulthood and education. That is, there is a form of religiousness whose shape is related to a world where strong, rational individuals are valued. There is also a religiousness which emerges from the interplay of the human generations and the relation of humans to non-humans. Both forms can make a claim to be adult, but I will try to show that the second is more comprehensive and also that from an educational perspective it is the more appropriate.

The word "religious" has a difficult time being combined with the noun "education." In the twentieth-century United States there have been two distinct and contrasting strands of religious education. On the one hand, religious education is understood to be the transmission of the Christian faith to children. For most Protestant churches either "Christian Education" is interchangeable with religious education or "Christian Education" is thought to be preferable because it is concretely descriptive of the educational task.

The other strand of meaning in the twentieth century has roots in the same evangelical tradition. But in this case writers back away from the narrowness of equating Christian beliefs and religion. A host of writers in the early part of the century moved away from the concrete objects of Bible and church while trying to assert the importance of religion. John Dewey and G. Stanley Hall were two of the most influential men in this group. Not surprisingly, John Dewey gave the keynote address at the first meeting of the Religious Education Association in 1903.[1] For these scholars religion is a quality of all experience which implies that all education is religious.

The comprehension of the second strand is at the expense of the concreteness in the first. If all education is religious education, is not the adjective simply redundant? The answer is yes unless a particular and concrete form can be assigned to the word "religious." That is, an adequate meaning of religious would have to incorporate both the demand for particularity and the drive toward what is universal. Religious can neither be a set of objects possessed by one group nor a vague, undifferentiated quality suffusing everything; in both cases "religious education" tends to disappear.

The movement toward a generalized religiousness made some sense in the early part of the century. Writers were trying to escape from an aggressive and dominant evangelism. But the ecumenical age of the late twentieth century requires a more solid substitute. The particular cannot be sacrificed to the general; instead, the particular has to be related to the universal. Religious education is the maintaining of a tension between particular and universal.

In trying to describe a meaning for the word "religious," we need a starting point that is almost beyond debate. That place, I suggest, is in a distinction between ordinary and non-ordinary. Every group has a sense of what is ordinary, habitual, and expected. Long before scientific laws were invented or discovered people had a sense of order and of what to expect. No group of people could exist together without an agreed-upon world. To live in the world is to experience an ordering.

Not every group experiences the same ordinary. What is ordinary in twentieth-century United States might be non-ordinary in a South Pacific island and vice versa. There are different ordinaries, but each group has some meaning for ordinary and also some awareness of what is not ordinary. Every group knows that there are some people at some time who represent the non-ordinary. One of the most universal events that is not ordinary is death. No one includes death as part of his or her ordinary day. The death of a human being has always awakened a sense that the orderliness of the everyday can be overturned. Other transitions in life, including birth, also appear as non-ordinary. They place humans "in touch with" some greater power than do the habitual processes of everyday life.

The fact that what is ordinary for one group is non-ordinary for another raises an issue that is crucial for religious life. The question is especially pertinent when the groups referred to are at earlier and later periods of history. Is the non-ordinary a realm that is constantly in retreat before the human power to order and control? Is there a clear and single direction to "modernization" so that what is non-ordinary for a backward group moves toward becoming ordinary for an advanced group? During the last two centuries of Western history the answer to that question has been yes. What I wish to do here is to propose an image for the relation of ordinary/non-ordinary that allows for another look at the question. The burden of proof is then placed upon those who assume that the human story moves in a single line of "progress."

The first image of ordinary and non-ordinary is the one assumed by the modern West. There are two areas whose sizes are inversely related.

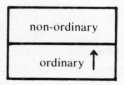

Ordinary and non-ordinary function as adjectives qualifying a noun; for example, object, time, space, or world. Religion becomes almost coextensive with the world of the non-ordinary or at least whatever is religion is located within the non-ordinary world. Trivial happenings out of the ordinary are not called "religious" and "religious" may be restricted to what is thought to be good so that the bad or evil side of the non-ordinary is antireligious. The religious part of the non-ordinary is called "the sacred"; its correlate, the ordinary world, is profane which means outside the sacred.

The almost inevitable direction in this image is up and down. The sacred is above the profane, and sacred, holy, or divine beings come down into ordinary human affairs. Within this picture the movement of human reason, that is, the power to order and control, is imagined to be a rebellion against power from on high. Every victory for humans below is a defeat for whatever is above. The world becomes progressively less mysterious with the advance of history.

The other image to relate the words "ordinary" and "non-ordinary" does not segregate them into two realms. Ordinary and non-ordinary do not describe objects but are instead aspects of a relational matrix. Here, qualitative change is important and one speaks of degrees, especially degrees of depth. This image is necessarily more complex than the first.

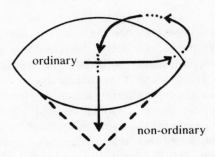

[1b]

The movement is not simply up and down but rather: out, over, back, down. The movement returns to where one began but at a deeper level and then the pattern can be repeated. A person doesn't pass once in a lifetime to a non-ordinary world; instead, the person moves constantly toward some center that always eludes a clear location. Religious is not coextensive with non-ordinary or exclusive of the ordinary. Moving "beyond the ordinary" is intrinsic to the religious journey, but one never actually leaves behind or leaves out the ordinary.

This idea of "going beyond" brings up a standard terminology found in modern Christian theology. The words "transcendence" and "immanence" appear frequently and are often used as if their meanings were obvious. However, if they are used in what appears to be their obvious literal meanings, they throw us into the first image. That is, "transcend" is a spatial image and though the spatial cannot be avoided, its misleading character has to be resisted. The supposition that there is a realm "beyond man" or "beyond human experience" is likely to be imagined as:

"transcendent"
Ordinary within human experience

[1c]

The image is reinforced when the word "transcendent" is used as a noun, as if "the transcendent" were a name for God.

In the second image the ordinary is transcended insofar as one cannot avoid using a spatial image. I have resisted the simplistic spatial connotation by describing the movement as out, over, back, and down. "Going beyond" and "going deeper within" are aspects of the same movement. A concern with the furthest reaches and the greatest depths of human experience is not a concern with the "merely immanent." The words "transcendent" and "immanent" are not played off against each other. Transcendent/immanent is a describing of experience. According to this image, if God is to be found, it is in the transcending-immanentizing journey.[2]

The two images I have drawn reflect two forms of religious-ness operative in the contemporary world. Actually, each of the two images breaks down into two variations. The first image with its strong up-and-down movement lends itself to a powerful form of religion in which the sacred comes down into human life. Here religion is filled with awe, reverence, and devotion. Not very far away, however, is a religion or quasi-religion in which the "up" takes precedence. Here religion takes on a "secular" form and the sacred becomes a competitor to be overcome.

In the second image there can be an undeveloped religious-ness in which individuals or groups have not yet explored the limits of human life. There can also be a religious form which incorporates the explorations of human reason and the movements of up and down. Thus, the second image can both precede and succeed the first. A fully developed religious image would combine the mature form of #2 and the better interpreta-tion of #1. The choice is not between right and wrong images but between images that are more or less adequate for interpreting religious life.

The two images correspond to the two ideals of adulthood. The two variations in the first image are both germane to the idea of the rational, objective individual. In discussing the second image I am interested in a fully developed form and not the primi-tive form. The claim I make is that this journey out, over, back, and down is appropriate to an ideal of adulthood that moves toward a unity of rational/non-rational, dependent/independent, human/non-human.

For contrasting the two forms of religiousness I will use six points of comparison. There is an arbitrariness to the number six, but there is consistency within each set of six. The six points I will use for my comments are:

#1	#2
1. Individual	1. Communal
2. Discursive speech	2. Rite, Paradox, Silence
3. Temporal points	3. Presence
4. Space	4. Place
5. Serious	5. Irony
6. Death at end	6. Life/Death/Life

In the course of my two descriptions the preference for #2 will be apparent. I would insist, nevertheless, that there is a truth to #1. The importance of individuality, discursive speech, temporal points, space, seriousness of life, and death at the end is not denied. The question is whether these characteristics can be maintained without a context provided by #2.

Form #1

[2a]

1. Individual

In this form of religiousness there is an acute consciousness of the individual. Though the ultimate intent of the journey may be the absorption of the individual into something greater than itself, the individual stands out. A rational ideal plays a key role even if the rational is eventually topped. The mind searches for life's answer and finally not finding it comes to the limit of rational control. Then "natural reason" is surpassed by "right reason" or reason is surpassed by faith.

The paradox here is the strongly individualistic bent of religions which call for submission of the individual to God. But, as Bernard Wishy points out in his study of nineteenth-century child rearing, preparing children to turn over their lives to God has the unintended effect of creating self-absorbed children.[3] Then the stress has to be on the "will" and its power to reverse the direction of life. The great revivalist Dwight Moody could use as his theme: "It is 'I will' or 'I won't' for every man in this hall tonight. . . . The battle is in the will and only there."[4] For the nineteenth-century boy this willing meant decisive action; for the girl it meant submission and acceptance.[5]

After one has "left one's mind," there is need for someone or something to accept the individual. Religious institutions and religious ideologies can be very powerful and extremely rigid. The individual who has been converted sees this rigidity as an advantage. The burden has been taken from the individual; the only struggle remaining is to keep one's will in the right direction. The religious revival of the 1950s which brought people back to church and religion in the 1970s which was often antiecclesiastical may not be so different as they would first appear. The church which functioned as recipient of individuals may have been replaced by other systems or gurus in the same role.

The popularity of Eastern gurus in the United States is not a recent phenomenon. A mysticism that lifts the individual out of the materialistic culture has always been an element in United States history. Individualism and anti-individualism are only a moment's decision apart so that techniques of Eastern religions can easily be put at the service of Western individualism.[6]

The absorption in God who receives the individual can suddenly seem to become a religion of the individual. In the eighteenth century Jonathan Edwards wrote in awe about the surprising and wonderful works of God. The revival was an unexpected grace coming down from God. A century later Charles Finney could say that "a revival of religion is not a miracle. There is nothing in religion beyond the ordinary powers of nature." The laws of human and divine psychology were now so well known, thought Finney, that ministers no longer had to "pray down" a revival but could "work one up whenever they chose."[7] This change of tone is ominous and prefigures further developments in revivalism throughout the nineteenth and twentieth centuries. the Rev. Horatio Alger would later take up advising individuals on how to be successful in his books that sold 200 million copies. A direct line runs from that literature to titles of a century later: *Power and How to Get It, Looking Out for No. 1, How to Be Your Own Best Friend*.

2. Discursive Speech

[2b]

In this religious form language is used as discourse. Long speeches combine careful logic and an accompanying appeal to the emotions. Two distinct functions are served by speech: bringing the individual within the system of truth and seeing that the system of truth is constantly reinforced.

Everything here has to be *said*. Persons who are in positions of authority have to maintain a constant check that no falsehoods are spoken and that there are no deviations from prescribed texts. A sermon is the ritual reinforcement of the texts for a group. The first and sometimes the only question is the truth. And the truth is in carefully formulated propositions.

Orthodoxy assumes great importance in this context. Education will be judged by whether the learners know the right beliefs that constitute the orthodox position. If the truth is available only through these texts and words, then the suppression of heresy is understandable. A questioning of any part of the system threatens the whole system. The former Cardinal of Boston, Richard O'Connell, once wrote to Francis Spellman: "It is something to have written and spoken for almost 50 years and never to have spoken or written a sentence that is not perfectly orthodox."[8] The fact is indeed remarkable, but one has to ask whether for a teacher the accomplishment is either possible or desirable.

3. Temporal Points

[2c]

A people's image of time is closely related to their religious life. When religion is the ascent of the individual or the descent of God, time is likely to be a series of points along the way. The past is "behind us" and the future is "before us." The individual strives toward the freedom of the future and away from the bondage of the past.

The presumption here is that individuals can change their lives and leave behind the past. The most important thing is to live in the *now* and choose the future one wishes. In an earlier Christian version God's grace was the force that renewed the world and opened the future. In the secular version the burden of constituting the future passed over to human decisions, but the hopes ran as high. Saint-Simon could say in 1814 that "the Golden Age of the human species is not behind us, it is before us."[9]

The United States, having been established in the period when this universal and progressive vision of history was envisioned, is strongly affected by this image of time. Tom Paine's sentiment that "we have it in our power to begin the world over again" was simply an echo of the colonial history and United States history on either side of him.[10] Despite disappointments United States history remains directed to the future where life will be better for our children. The children are revered because they represent the future and they are out in front of the adults when it comes to understanding the future that is breaking in on us.[11] The past has little to offer except a memory of when life was simpler. The past is disregarded, but it keeps recurring in fits of nostalgia. "Having, as it were, lost the past from our present, we look back on it fondly, and so often vapidly."[12]

4. Space

[2d]

Space in this religious image is of crucial importance. One could say that the previous description of time is a spatial image insofar as time is imagined to be a series of points along a line. There is no escape from spatial images, but space needs examination lest its infinitelike appearance be identified with the fullness humans search for.

Space can be alluring. A sacred space above and beyond ordinary space gives stability to life with its constant flux. In earlier religions the space may have been consecrated "at the beginning of time." Mysterious parts of the natural world or sections of the temple were spots that the gods inhabited.[13]

In the modern secular version space is still attractive but now as something to be conquered. With the gods in retreat, space means openness and possibility. Not surprisingly, the history of the United States is marked by the conquest of space. The movement from East coast to West coast was followed by a reaching out to the rest of the earth and then to the stars. Since the United States trusts above all in each individual having private space, there is always a fear that the country is running out of room even though the country as a whole is underpopulated.

5. Serious

[2e]

A distinguishing note in this kind of religion is the deadpan seriousness with which the individual strives for salvation. Playfulness and humor are suspect and making fun of sacred things is blasphemous. The chief literary form is the hero myth in which an individual sets his or her mind and conquers evil.

The seriousness of the search for salvation is a theme connecting all the previous points. Systems of belief have no room for playing with language. And if time is passing at the rate of 60 seconds per minute, one must devote all of one's attention to spending it wisely. One popular manual on "managing" your life and marriage advises that time given to future and past is "time lost in the vital present. And the loss of that present time cuts down on your awareness of what is happening between you and your mate."[14]

The words which signal seriousness are "awareness" and "consciousness." There is a "consciousness industry" in the United States which advises people on using every moment effectively if they wish to have perfect marriages, brilliant children, and superior orgasms. Edwin Schur scathingly criticizes this industry: "It appeals almost exclusively to the middle and upper classes, it is politically innocuous and socially complacent, and it is being promoted and marketed in the best Madison Avenue tradition."[15] Although Schur's criticism may be accurate, I think his conclusion is misleading: "It has become the new civic religion of the U.S." Actually, all the elements go back to colonial days and had coalesced by the nineteenth century. The numerous books today that claim "You are the sum of your choices" are reworking the theme of the nineteenth-century McGuffey readers: "Where there's a will, there's a way" and "If at first you don't succeed, try, try again."[16]

The problem is not that life isn't serious. Serious attacks on seriousness won't change much. The problem is that solemn advice-givers don't seem to recognize how bad things can get. "The human condition may be desperate," wrote Albert Camus, "but it is not unequivocally serious." Visionaries throughout the centuries have seen how deadly serious life can be, but they have borne the vision not mainly by heightening their consciousness but by having a greater world as the context of their individual consciousness.

6. *Death at End*

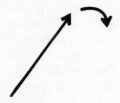

[2f]

Where life is a series of points to be mastered, death appears as the last point that upsets the scheme. Where life is conceived as an expansion of consciousness, death is a very depressing fact. Two responses are possible: Either true consciousness follows death or else death is final but can be put out of sight until it arrives. What joins these two responses is that attention is riveted on the *now* when salvation alone can be gained.

At earlier periods of United States history death was difficult to forget for long. A high death rate for children remained well into the nineteenth century. The old died close to home and many diseases could suddenly spread. Although death could seem like a cruel joke, religion gave comfort with belief in life after death. A person could concentrate on preparing for a "happy death."[17]

The modern image keeps the movement upward, but it no longer looks toward true life after death. Man was supposed to attain salvation in this life by his own efforts at mastery. The "skull which grins at the table" (William James) had to be put out of sight and out of consciousness. But being placed outside consciousness does not eliminate the problem. Death works in darker caverns of the human psyche and comes to light in lurid phantasy and a taste for violence. An obsession with death is never far from a consciousness which speaks exclusively of life.

The contemporary concern with death does not necessarily mean a change in this regard. Much of the interest in death is in technique and detail. The individual is now being called to master the problem of death. Jacob Needleman writes: "Death preoccupies us without compelling us to feel our lack of knowing who and what we are, and in what world we exist. Having been lost in the illusion that we stand over against the whole universe, we now believe we can come to grips with death merely by thinking about it."[18]

Summary

This religious image which speaks of "God and man" tries to lift the individual out of egocenteredness. The linguistic currency it uses, however, may not be adequate to its intention. Karl Barth used to say: "One does not say God by saying man in a loud voice." While that is true, neither does one say God by saying man in a low voice.[19] The real difficulty is that neither God nor man is available for choice. God is mediated through objects of experience and "man" is not the name of anyone. In fact, "man" can be a dangerous abstraction. "Man is the ideology of dehumanization" (Theodor Adorno).

What actually seems to happen is that individual men (not man) try to appropriate the means of salvation. The control is spoken of in the name of God, but, strangely enough, God and man can substitute for one another. There has been easy passage in United States history between God-centered, other-worldly religion and a this-worldly religion of man. We do not get beyond a religion of man by urging God as a choice beyond man. The first step is to challenge the language and imagery of this religion as individualistic, sexist, and antiecological. The alternative to God above man is a search for religious meaning in the interplay of men, women, children, and others.

Form #2

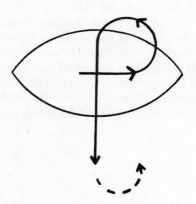

[3]

This second image is intended to convey a meaning of religiousness that can encompass more than the first image. This meaning is not more general or abstract; it is just as particular and concrete as the first. In fact, this second image takes a form that is more earthy, bodily, and personal than a religion which speaks of "God and man." As I have acknowledged, this image can describe what is called "primitive" religiousness. However, it is also capable of including the best impulses of the first image and thereby of describing a "postmodern" form of religiousness. This latter possibility is what I explore in the following six points.

1. Communal

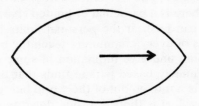

[3a]

The word "communal" refers to the relation of person and intimate group. For ancient peoples the emphasis seems to have been on the tribe or other collective forms. Over a period of thousands of years and especially in recent centuries the individual emerged in contrast to the group. This step could represent progress for the human race, but the development does pose a dangerous problem. A cult of the individual has unfortunate side effects for infants, old people, sick people, and others who do not fit the ideal of the strong, rationally controlled individual.

The sense of human group preceded modern individualism and that sense has never been entirely displaced. Today there is renewed interest in national, ethnic, racial, and religious groupings. Some of this interest may be dangerous and much of it is a passing fad. But the recognition of human groupings is simply an admission of an elementary fact of life. The human journey is taken by an individual, but he or she starts from a physical, psychic, and social relation with a small group of people. Some of the effects of primary groupings never leave us throughout the transformations of our lives.

A communal group provides the material with which we work and sometimes against which we struggle. The paradox of life is that the realities which limit us are the realities which sustain us. Religiously, we need the discipline of a group of intimates "who demand of us that we be not less than ordinary men and women fulfilling our ordinary experience. For if we are not at least this, how can we hope to be more?"[20]

As one struggles to be free of the parochialism of a group one discovers that there is a parochial or limited character to oneself. The individual can push at the personal limits but not dissolve them. The limits of every community teach the person the meaning of human limit and give intimation of some greater community. The communally based person finds that the way to transcend finiteness is not to go out of the world but to go through the world. The individual is flipped upside down to continue a journey toward the center of the earth.

2. Rite, Paradox, Silence

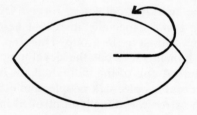

[3b]

The form of communication which brings the person to the center of the community is ritual, that is, non-verbal gesture which both expresses the life of a people and also points beyond the small group. In this religious image most of the meaning is left unsaid. When speech is used, the poetic and the paradoxical take precedence. The non-ordinary is not in an added realm which can be described in (ordinary) speech. When the non-ordinary is discovered at the limits of the personal/communal, there is no way one can directly describe it. Images and symbols embody the meaning; rituals such as stories, sex, diet, and games provide experience of the rational and more than rational.

The most striking characteristic of speech used for religious purposes is the double negative. How does one affirm the non-ordinary when all words are ordinary? The answer requires four steps: 1) Affirm the ordinary; 2) Recognize the limit (or negation) of the ordinary; 3) Refuse to accept (negate) that limit (negation) as final; 4) One therefore affirms the non-ordinary by negating the negations of the ordinary. Religious statements follow the dictum of Emily Dickinson: "Tell the truth but tell it slant."

Even to say "God exists," is, if not false, a misleading statement. Grammatically it says that there is an object (God) which stands out (e-xists) among other objects. No one trying to convey religious meaning would wish to use so reductive a statement. Of course, the sentence "God does not exist" is also misleading and could be interpreted as simple atheism. What one can say is that "God does not not exist" which affirms a meaning for God by challenging the limits we have placed on what it means "to be." At the least the sentence jolts us into awareness that there may be other meanings to religious statements than either (*a*) emotional effusions or (*b*) an attempt to describe a world outside and above the ordinary world.

This reflection may give some solace to religion teachers who find that their words fail them. They should hardly be surprised. Religion is not a "content" which can be given to another person. If there is one thing which joins Eastern and Western masters of religion, it is their use of paradox. The Christian Bible, for example, is filled with peculiar sayings, strange stories, and puzzling forms of literature. J. Dominic Crossan has shown that the parables of Jesus are forms of speaking that start from the very ordinary and then bend back on themselves. In Crossan's scheme, parables undercut the myths which precede them; in my terms, parables negate the negations of existing religious stories.[21]

The double negative is followed by silence. All speech must end in silence, but the silence can be empty or profound.[22] As the curved line indicates, the silence is at the middle of the community and the middle of speech. The "edge of language" is sometimes imagined to be a wall or seacoast, but these images are misleading. Religious silence is not over a wall but in the deeper life of the community. Speech arises constantly from that well of silence and when one is finally left speechless in ecstasy or sorrow, a silence that is full is at the center of things.

3. Presence

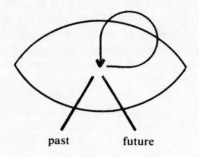

past   future

[3c]

Time is here imagined not as before us and behind us but underneath us. We literally stand on the shoulders of the past and the future is what comes from gently reshaping the past. As in the first image, the present is all there is, but here present does not mean a moment always disappearing. Present is what a person is to other humans and non-humans; that is, presence to others enables us to discover the riches of the past and the possibilities of a future.

Ancient peoples had not yet discovered or invented the future. They lived in the present with what the past had deposited. There was movement of time, but it was not a straight line that went forward and up. However, the assumption that our choice is between circles and straight lines has to be rejected. Circles and straight lines are both figures of points in sequence. The alternative to both circles and straight lines is a sphere. There is a sense in which time goes by bit by bit, but it actually never leaves us. In Samuel Beckett's striking image, time is the falling of grains of sand which lead finally to the earth coming up to meet us.[23]

The discovery or invention of the future could be a positive development within the sphere of time. Humans discovered that they had more possibilities than they had previously imagined. As humans managed to change things to their liking, the category of future came to exist. The future, like the related concept "the individual," can become an obsession which distracts humans from the present. Books are always asking rhetorically "must we not think more of the future than of the present and past?"²⁴ My answer is: no. We ought to think more of the future in relation to the past and the way to do that is by living more profoundly in the present.

4. Place

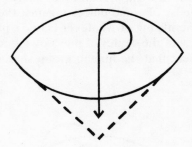

[3d]

The religious attitude of a people is always embodied somewhere. The community consists of human bodies and of earth which surrounds them. From ancient times the dead have been placed in the earth so that people and earth became continuous. Place is where people live and the more they live there the more it is a place. Space is an abstract quality or an object that individuals master. Place is a human setting that a people tend, care, and love. For ancient people everything had its place; things were sacred because they were in the right place.²⁵

In much of modern history it was thought that the sacredness of place was a childish trait. Now there is a growing suspicion that the "primitive" outlook may also be the progressive one. Tractors, fertilizers, mines, and oil wells may temporarily increase human well being. But humans cannot treat the goods of the earth exploitatively or else the earth will take its revenge. Reverence toward earth, air, and water is returning to center stage in the quest for survival and progress.

Presence and place go together just as temporal points and

space make up a pair. A religious life that is to include the past also has to be a religion of place. Christian theology often claims that the religious choice is between the God of time and the gods of space. That is not quite accurate. The choice is between a god of time/space and (a) god(s) of tradition/place. "Sacred places" need not be understood in a primitivistic way. Modern mobility, for example, does not necessarily destroy a sense of place; it could even increase one's appreciation of many places. The issue is not the sacredness of some places (against the profaneness of others) but the sacralizing of whatever is one's place. Today that means a discovery of the center of one's own body and a respect for the environment that the human group shares with others.[26]

5. Irony

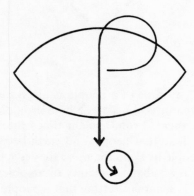

[3e]

    As the religious person gets a sense of unfathomable mystery, the response is comic irony. Not that life isn't serious. It is just that the mystery and complexity are so far beyond our serious efforts one has to laugh. Our most elaborate theories finally fail to explain anything. Our most intense efforts to master the universe are destined for extinction.

    Comic irony is perilously close to total despair. The difference is that the undercutting of language occurs within a context that defines irony. Non-verbal rites provide a solidarity with the universe; experience of a community gives a sense of identity.

Human individuals tend to exaggerate themselves out of all proportion. The two ways to be brought back to earth (*humus*) are by *hum*ility and *hum*or. Humility is the preferred way for individuals in the first image. Humor is the way in a religion of tradition and community.[27]

Irony makes us see how small and powerless we are. But religious irony places us at the center where size and power are seen to be less important. One of Beckett's characters, Malone, says: "The loss of consciousness was for me never a great loss." The line is ridiculous, but it undercuts the deadly serious talk about heightening one's consciousness. In the end we all lose consciousness, so what's the point of all the struggle?

Irony is a form of the double negative. The ordinary is affirmed but not without a twist that makes us see a bit of the ridiculous in everything. Thus, even consciousness, the humans' claim to fame, can be made fun of. The human ego needs to be thrown into relief against some overpowering reality. The first religious impulse, says Max Scheler, is "Thou All, I Nothing." The second moment is "Thou All, I not quite nothing." The human is recognized in irony as "not quite nothing," which in this religious image is to give high praise.[28]

6. *Life/Death/Life*

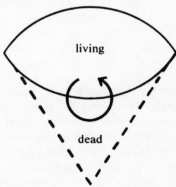

[3f]

An interpretation of death follows from all of the preceding elements. Death is always a communal affair involving individuals in relation to a group. Death demands ritual and eventually silence. Death is a way of taking up a new mode of presence in the body and earth of the community. Death is also choice material for comic irony. In this image death is neither an obsession throughout life nor a cruel surprise at the end of life. Death is a peculiar character one has to allow into daily life.

From the standpoint of both community and environment death is not in some other realm outside the ordinary. Dying is a part of a cycle that is always operating. The community of humans receives new members each day and buries other members each day. Humans survive at all only because of an unimaginably complex cycle of life and death. Everything in and of the earth participates in the double movement of life toward death and death toward life. The humans are distinctive by looking more deeply into the meaning of this process.

The cycle of life and death is not a closed circle. At least some of the movement is life-death-greater life. One sees that movement in the interplay of mineral-vegetable-animal life. Within human life the little deaths along the way open the door to greater life. A lifetime of experience prepares the way for trusting that what is called "death" is entrance into a new life which is beyond our imagination. The ultimate religious conviction is in the form of a double negative: Love, care, and devotion do not count for nothing.

Summary

The religious image that has been described is most closely represented by a sphere. Prophets and poets constantly return to the image of God at the center with the human being an "eccentric particle."[29] The temptation of humans with their hierarchical misconceptions is to disdain help "from below" and to try to escape to a perch above the fray. What they need is to establish a partnership with non-human friends on the earth and non-living humans in the earth. The route of the journey is then revealed: "The saint goes to the center, the poet and the artist to the ring where everything comes round again."[30]

The route of the journey implies that the non-ordinary is discovered in the ordinary itself. We come back home and discover it for the first time. The non-ordinary was under our feet all the time, but we hadn't noticed it. A danger in contemporary religious movements is the failure to appreciate the ordinary. One has to have a sense of rootedness and embodied humanness before one tries to transcend any limits.[31] Then the attaining of a great vision will not lead to a renouncing or hating of our ordinary selves. Writing of Hasidism, Paul Lacey says: "One puts off the habitual but not repudiates it; when the habitual is seen afresh, it testifies to the holy."[32]

If "God is all in all" and yet each thing has its place and relative autonomy, then certain educational principles follow. First, it is important to have a sense of awe and mystery before one begins educational examination. Second, nothing of ordinary experience is immediately to be excluded from the material of religious education; at the same time a careful attention to the limits of the ordinary is needed if the education is to be religious. Third, it is crucial to provide an adequate setting for the whole dangerous journey. If religious education does in fact occur, that means a person goes out of his or her mind to plumb the depths of the ordinary and then come home again. In the next chapter we examine the family/community as the human setting in which the individual's journey takes place.

Notes

1. John Dewey, "Religious Education as Conditioned by Modern Psychology and Pedagogy," *Religious Education*, 69(Jan./Feb., 1974), pp. 5–11: A reprint of the first annual convention of the Religious Education Association, 1903; see also Joseph Kett, *Rites of Passage* (New York, Basic, 1977), pp. 204f.

2. See Paul Tillich, *Systematic Theology*, Vol. I (Chicago, University of Chicago, 1951), p. 163.

3. Bernard Wishy, *The Child and the Republic* (Philadelphia, University of Pennsylvania, 1968), p. 19.

4. See Bernard Weisberger, *They Gathered at the River* (Boston, Little, Brown and Co., 1958), p. 211.

5. See Kett, *op.cit.* p. 75.

6. See Harvey Cox, *Turning East* (New York, Simon and Schuster, 1977).

7. Charles Finney, "What a Revival of Religion Is," in *The American Evangelicals*, ed. William McLoughlin (New York, Harper, 1968), pp. 86–100.

8. John Deedy, "William Henry O'Connell: The Prince of Yesterday's Prototypes," *Critic*, Summer 1977, pp. 54–61.

9. Quoted in Frank Manuel, *Shapes of Philosophical History* (Stanford, Stanford University, 1965), p. 102.

10. See Henry May, *The Enlightenment in America* (New York, Oxford, 1976), p. 163.

11. See Warren Bennis and Philip Slater, *The Temporary Society* (New York, Harper Colophon, 1968), pp. 20–52.

12. Robert Nisbet, *Twilight of Authority* (New York, Oxford, 1975), pp. 89f.

13. See Mircea Eliade, *Cosmos and History* (New York, Harper Torchbook, 1959) on sacred space; see also on the danger of spatial metaphors, C. E. Rolt, *Dionysius Areopagita on the Divine Names and the Mystical Theology* (New York, Macmillan, 1940), introduction.

14. George O'Neill and Nena O'Neill, *Open Marriage* (Philadelphia, Lippincott, 1972), p. 79.

15. Edwin Schur, *The Awareness Trap* (New York, Quadrangle, 1976), p. 77.

16. See Louis Wright, *Culture on the Moving Frontier* (Bloomington, University of Indiana, 1955), p. 215.

17. See David Stannard, *The Puritan Way of Death* (New York, Oxford, 1977).

18. Jacob Needleman, *A Sense of the Cosmos* (Garden City, Doubleday, 1975), p. 57.

19. See Roger Hazelton, *Ascending Flame, Descending Dove* (Philadelphia, Westminister, 1975), p. 105.

20. A. C. Robin Skynner, "The Relationship of Psychotherapy and Sacred Tradition," in *On the Way to Self Knowledge*, ed. Jacob Needleman and Dennis Lewis (New York, Knopf, 1976), p. 224.

21. See John Dominic Crossan, *The Dark Interval* (Chicago, Argus, 1975).

22. See William Johnston, *Silent Music* (New York, Harper and Row, 1974), p. 56: "It is well said in Japan that any clown can tell the difference between wise talk and foolish talk; but it takes a good master to distinguish between wise silence and foolish silence."

23. See Richard Gilman, *The Making of Modern Drama* (New York, Farrar, Straus, Giroux, 1974), pp. 234–66.

24. Karl Rahner, *The Shape of the Church to Come* (New York, Seabury, 1974), p. 27.

25. See Bruno Bettelheim, *The Uses of Enchantment* (New York, Knopf, 1976), p. 23.

26. See Vine DeLoria, *God Is Red* (New York, Grosset and Dunlap, 1973).

27. See James Hillman, "Peaks and Vales," in *On the Way to Self Knowledge,* ed. Jacob Needleman and Dennis Lewis (New York, Knopf, 1976), p. 127.

28. See Monica Furlong, *The End of Our Exploring* (New York, Coward, 1974), pp. 168–70; Hugo Rahner, *Man at Play* (New York, Herder and Herder, 1967), p. 29.

29. Joseph Miller, *Poets of Reality* (Cambridge, Harvard, 1966), p. 281.

30. William B. Yeats as quoted in James Olney, *Metaphors of Self* (Princeton, University of Princeton, 1972), p. 47.

31. See Amos Wilder, *Theopoetic: Theology and the Religious Imagination* (Philadelphia, Fortress, 1976), p. 19.

32. Quoted in Sallie Teselle, *Speaking in Parables* (Philadelphia, Fortress, 1975), p. 116.

5. The Family in Educational Context

Chapter Three presented an educational model which distinguished between a schooling and a laboratory form of learning. One of the three elements in the laboratory was family/community which was reserved until now for extended treatment. Family/community deserves special consideration both because of its importance and because of confusion that surrounds the topic today. During the past fifteen years there has been an explosion of writing on the history and current state of the family.

A problem with much of this writing is that if authors choose to study the family, they are liable to have already mistaken the question. The constant reference in this book to family/community is an attempt to provide a workable base from which to begin. My interest is in the relation of family to its environment and especially its relation to non-familial but personal forms of organization. Those relationships are the place where crucial changes can occur and are occurring today. As for the family itself, I will offer this simple but perhaps startling thesis: What we now mean by family is a unit that has not changed much over the centuries and in all likelihood will not change much in the future.

My thesis runs counter to two bodies of literature that currently attract much attention. There is a group of people who bewail the collapse of the family and are demanding a restoration of the old ways. There is another group of people who think that the family needs replacement and would applaud a dissolution of old ways. These two groups do agree on one thing, namely, that the existing family is a poor image of an ideal family that either until recently did exist (conservative defenders) or will suddenly be invented in the future (radical opponents). I think both sides are blind to what is in front of their eyes: the family continuing to exist as it has in the past. There is not the slightest evidence that anything is about to replace the family. So long as the human race continues, that is, so long as there are children, the family will be there as it has been.

The reader may feel that I have stated a thesis which is based only on verbal finesse. By restricting the meaning of family to its current focus on parent and child I can claim that the family has changed little. I admit that one can start with a different meaning of family and then find that considerable change has occurred. However, my way of stating the question will locate precisely where change has occurred and will clarify what has to be done in the future.

Debate over the family often takes place within assumptions that need examining. One of those assumptions is the ideal of adulthood. As I have described in Chapters Two, Three, and Four, there are two competing ideals of adulthood that operate in United States society. The assumption of the first ideal (the adult is a rational, objective, productive individual) runs into difficulty when related to the family. In this chapter I will first describe what happens when this ideal of adulthood governs the discussion of the family. Then I will turn to the second ideal of adulthood (the degree of integration reached by a person reconciling the tension of rational/non-rational, dependent/independent, life/death). I will pick up some help from the premodern period of family and then describe a contemporary model for relating familial and non-familial forms of community life.

The situation of the family throughout most of United States history could be diagrammed this way (f=father, m=mother, and c=child):

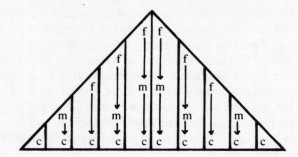

[1a]

The picture represents a pyramidic structure of economic and political power. The family helps to define that structure and is in turn influenced by it. Some characteristics of family life follow directly from this picture:

1. Power

The flow of power here is up and down. Authority is maintained by the exercise of control from above and obedience from below. The father was the head of the family and in his absence the mother ruled.[1] Most state laws on family still reflect this image. Children did not have rights apart from adult authority. Child rearing in the United States has gone through regular cycles of strict and permissive, but the changes have not been as great as might first seem. Strict/permissive are variations within a unilateral flow of power.[2]

2. Sexuality

Sexual expression would follow the same lines as power in this diagram. Sexual life is under the control of the male. Periodically sex may spill over the top of this diagram in forms beyond marriage. Society is tolerant of the occasionally erring male. The woman is submissive to the man and not thought to be very interested in sex. Any sexual expression for the woman outside marriage would be promiscuous. Whereas the hero in United

States literature was a male whose sex life is segmented from his person, the heroine has been a woman who did not reach sexual maturity.[3] The child's sex life is carefully controlled though in practice there is often a tolerance (and possibly envy) of youthful escapades.

3. Work

The father in this picture is the "breadwinner," the one whose work in field or factory provided for the sustenance of the family. The mother worked, too, but with the coming of the Industrial Revolution her sphere was not called "work." Young women still flocked to factory and shop, but the hope was to escape from there to home and family. The woman who remained working in the mill was forever a "spinster," not generally a happy fate. The child had had a subordinate role in economic production which was almost completely eliminated in the nineteenth century. Laws were passed to keep children out of work and in school.

4. Incomplete Families

The diagram suggests that not all families included father/mother/children, but that there is little provision for these cases. If the role of each person is defined by the relation of father to mother to children, then the absence of one of those elements could be calamitous. Obviously, this situation occurs quite often. Death and divorce are the most common reasons for the absence of a parent. But even when neither of those things has occurred, the father in United States history has often been an absent figure—presumably at work.[4] The woman has often carried both roles, a theme one can see reflected in women's literature of the nineteenth century, popular plays, comic strips, and television of the twentieth century. The absence of the mother causes more havoc than the father's absence and few men were able to handle that family situation. The absence of children is also disruptive to this picture. Children are a burden to the mother but also her means of contact with people and institutions beyond the home.

For anyone who conceives of adulthood as living rationally, productively, and individually, this picture of the family presents severe restrictions. Only the male head of the family has any chance to be adult. But he may feel so weighted down by responsibilities that he may think he cannot live his own life. The children are not adults, but they (at least the boys) can look forward to some day being grown up. The one in the middle is the woman who seems doomed to be forever a dependent creature rather than an adult.

There have been recurrent feminist movements in United States history. The early nineteenth century, not surprisingly, produced a cry for women's equality just as work was passing from household to factory. The solution that carried the day was Catherine Beecher's position of "separate spheres" for men and women.[5] The woman's job was to tend the home and influence the children. The man's job was the separate but equal task of earning money outside the home. That truce was generally maintained into the twentieth century. Just below the surface, however, a problem continued to lurk, namely, that by the criteria of the society women were still not adults. The "spheres" were not equal when power, sex, and money were at stake.

The United States and much of the rest of the world have entered a new phase of feminist effort. Hardly anyone would now defend injustices and inequities that women have borne in the past. But there remains a real point of debate, which Alice Rossi pinpoints: "The sexual liberationist clearly rejects the traditional double standard; what is not clear is whether the new single standard will be modeled after what may have been the male pattern, the female pattern, or some amalgam of the two."[6] The double standard here refers not only to sex but also to power and money. Will women get some of that power position men have or will there be a new form for the exercise of power? Will women get access to the marketplace where the men have been or will work change its shape? Will women merely be free to go the male route of sex or will sex be reintegrated with life and work? The answers to these questions still hang in the balance.

What is clear in much writing today is a rebellion directed against the family but a rebellion that doesn't get free of family language. The literature is a parallel to antischool literature which has nowhere to go once it has equated school with education but is frustrated by the limits of school. As adult education literature contrasts school and self-directed learning, so also there is literature that pits the family against the self-directed individual. What would be helpful instead would be social forms that are not "alternative families" but complements to family life.

Attempts to tamper with the family run into a special problem. No one has the choice to be born or to be born into a specific family. People who wish to be independent and self-directed have to reckon with their own birth and childhood. Influences that precede individual choice form a base that is never left behind. The struggle to become an adult is often a contorted attempt to escape from the limitations of one's own childhood. The assumed ideal of adulthood which is functioning here needs to be challenged.

Before looking at a model of family/community appropriate to our second ideal of adulthood we must look back to an earlier period of family life. Similar to religious life a "postmodern" form of family/community includes what has been dismissed as "primitive." Before the Industrial Revolution the situation of the family might be pictured this way:

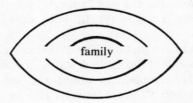

[1b]

The most important thing about this picture, which we have to restore, is that the family was at the center. The inner circle of father/mother/children easily spilled across to circles of friends, neighbors, servants, clients, and kinfolk. Much of the rest of society, including work and government, had some of the characteristics of family life. Lest this picture be romanticized, the "familialization" of politics was not necessarily better than modern political forms. A king conceived as a father figure might be doubly difficult to fight. The family served many roles from its central position including that of being the basic unit of production in the economy. The women were at home, but home was where the business economy was. A large number of children was an economic advantage because they were additional work hands.

During a period of many centuries the family was displaced from the center of production and the center of political life. One can best get a sense of this change by studying the family's relation to the city.[7] In premodern times the city had grown up as a center of political, economic, and domestic life. Those who were rich could maintain places outside the city and have the best of both worlds: the privacy and natural beauty of the "suburbs" and the power of the city's economic and political life. At first the family's position did not seem altered; families who could afford the suburbs were relocated for their own health. However, as great numbers of families followed the rich, both the city and the family changed. The paradox here is that everyone cannot move to the suburbs. If everyone moves out of the city, then there no longer is a city and *a fortiori* there aren't any suburbs.[8] One can continue to use the word "city" for devastated buildings and a trapped population; one can say "suburb" when one means endless sprawl along a highway. In both cases the terms are equivocal.

The process I have just described has been going on throughout the whole history of the United States. In fact, William Bradford was already complaining about the suburbanization of Plymouth in the 1640s.[9] Massachusetts Bay in the same decade tried to force workers to live within a short distance of where they worked. There is not much debate about the existence of this movement which took the family out of town and away from being the center of economic/political life. However, there is one glaring misuse of language that confuses the description of the process and thereby misunderstands the plight of the contemporary family. I refer to the phrase "nuclear family" and its paired phrase "extended family."

There is a regular argument which starts with someone making a contrast between the extended family of the past and the nuclear family of today. The date of the decline is variously assigned as mid-nineteenth century, the turn of the twentieth century, or post-World War II. Although the date is thought to be debatable, the fact of a change from extended to nuclear is assumed to be so obvious as not to need proof.

Such a statement about the recent origin of the nuclear family is then countered by a historian who says that history shows otherwise.[10] The nuclear family, it is said, goes back to the beginning of the colonies in North America and probably well before that. John Demos's study of Plymouth is most often cited in support of the seventeenth-century nuclear family and other studies can support the claim.[11]

The historian comes to this conclusion from studying art, architecture, marriage and birth records, information on town government and schools. The historian's data do not show a contrast of nuclear and extended families. For example, people who refer to the time when grandparents were regularly part of the household with parents and children are inventing a nostalgic fiction. Today less than 10 percent of grandparents live with their children and grandchildren, but that is probably not much different than at any time in United States history. The three-generation household has probably never been the norm in Western society.[12]

Although the historians have the data on their side, they never seem to win this argument. Statements about the extended family of the past and the nuclear family of the present are casually made in the press and on television every day. The historians' data are simply dismissed because "everybody knows" that some fundamental change has happened to the family. If it is nuclear today, it must have been extended in the past. The strange thing in this discussion is the failure to question whether nuclear and extended are appropriate adjectives to describe the family.

The first thing to note about the words "nuclear/extended" is that they are not a logical pair, as, for example, major/minor, producer/consumer, large/small. If we are to have a two-category system, we have to be sure that the two describe the possible alternatives. History and logic show that the contrast of nuclear and extended is misleading.

The word "nuclear" does convey a very definite image and one which is still important. A nucleus is the center of some circular or spherical figure. A "nuclear family" would be at the center of some structure. The alternative to "nuclear" is not extended but "eccentric." The failure to be at the center is precisely the problem of the contemporary family. The not so innocent irony is that "nuclear" is the most inappropriate metaphor for the family today.

The historian with a sense of this root meaning of nuclear argues for the existence of the nuclear family in seventeenth-century Massachusetts and England. But the historians fail to carry the argument through to conclusion: Not only did the nuclear family exist in the seventeenth century, but the nuclear family is precisely what does not exist today. If one separates the innermost circle from a series of concentric circles, one can call it many things but not a "nucleus."

What may seem like a minor point of imagery makes all the difference in the world when one tries to correct deficiencies or launch reforms. The worst condition you can suffer is to be in need of a cure whose appropriate name is the name everyone gives to your disease. Since it is endlessly repeated that the problem with the family is its nuclearity, then no one can propose to make the family nuclear again, that is, to resituate the family in the middle of things.

With the language and historical fiction surrounding the family it is assumed that the decreasing size of the household is the family's problem. Thus, we regularly have movements to "extend" the family by adding blood relatives or others to the household. Not surprisingly, an increase in the size of the household today usually has results that are innocuous or disastrous. If the contemporary family suffers by being outside the center of economic power, then simply adding numbers will probably worsen that problem.

For a variety of reasons family size did decrease in modern times. But that change was incidental to other changes and has little to do with the main problem of the family today. Adding members to household or family will not reverse the historical process which has affected family life. The family first became eccentric and then became isolated. The question for a contemporary model of family/community is how to restore the family to the center. How do we recover the ancient sense of centeredness but in a way that is realistic in our present world?[13]

The second half of this chapter can now describe a family/community model for the second ideal of adulthood. Major changes have occurred in individual and family life. I see no way in which the family can recover many of its lost functions, but that fact may not be bad news. The family could be freer to concentrate on its main function of providing for children. If it is to do that job, however, it needs to have its problem of environment or context adequately described and eventually changed. The family needs to return to the center, but it now has to share that center with other forms that are non-familial. It would be undesirable to return to a time when the center was entirely controlled by the family. At the center there should be non-familial communal forms which can cooperate with the family in challenging modern forms of organized power. For 98 percent of children the family remains *the* center of life, but for contemporary adults the family is only *one* of the ways of centering life.

The diagram below combines the good elements of premodern society and the indelible marks of modern life:

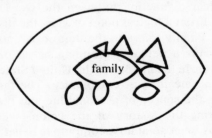

Family is one of the circles at the center. Other circles, presently to be named, exist next to the family or overlap the family. In addition there are pyramidic figures which arise from the family or exist on its boundaries. I do not expect that the modern corporate form will disappear. However, it might be brought under control by the family and its associates. That hope might seem quixotic except that change is occurring in the nature of work. As technology is miniaturized, work may return to the home; that is, as steel is replaced by plastic, the need for huge, segregated plants decreases; as work becomes more mental, a woman mathematician need not leave her family setting to go to work.[14]

There is one change that is certainly happening and is bound to affect sex, marriage, and family. I refer to the human race's getting control of the procreative process. For the first time in history adults with developed sexual lives are choosing whether or not to be parents. That change opens a new era in human history. We are only at the threshold of this era. If fewer adults become parents and parents have fewer children, what effect does that have on individuals and family structure? No one knows yet, but the change will be for ill unless the family has a supportive environment and unless there are forms of life which are non-familial but humanizing. Fewer adults in families might be good for the family if the adults becoming parents are people well prepared for the parental role. The data so far are not optimistic. Let's hope that we are merely in a transitional period because pregnancies are now on the rise in two groups: the poor who cannot get control of their lives and teenagers.[15]

The relation of familial and non-familial forms of community presumes a clear distinction between the words "family" and "community." From a logical point of view the distinction would seem obvious: Family refers to the unit of parents and children; community means a personal grouping based on some shared values. However, in the history of the United States, family tends to take over the meaning of community. The family is praised exorbitantly as the source of personal life and the answer to all problems. During the history of the colonies and the United States there has been an almost continuous belief that the family has just disintegrated.[16] Actually, the problem is almost the reverse. The family, far from disintegrating, has been almost the only thing standing. The family is such a topic of concern because it has *not* collapsed and can be seen to sag under the weight of its communal burden.

The word "community" has been overused to such an extent that it may be difficult to give any precise meaning to the term. The church is not the only institution that talks incessantly of community. Racial groups, politicians, and school systems do the same thing. One sometimes gets the impression that institutions use the word "community" whenever they are trying to obscure the real nature of their operation.

Despite the abuse of the word "community" a great issue is at stake in the word. Community refers to the communion of humans, that is, the unity in which human differences remain.[17] The differentiating of human uniqueness and the movement toward human solidarity occur together. There is no other available word to express this miraculous characteristic of the human being.

There is, of course, the word "love." But love is often restricted to two people and is used to refer to the feeling between them. Community refers to more than two and it includes the structure which holds people together. Community is not dependent on a feeling of romantic love but on an awareness of our common humanity. Each community is an intimation of a unity to which all human beings are called. Community requires some element of bonding that brings the members into intimate association and mutual exchange.

The family is the most obvious expression of community; its bond goes deep into biology and blood. Without some kind of family no one would make it through the first months of life. The family is the source of physical survival and psychological development for many years. Thus, the family is a necessary expression and probably the most important expression of community. Nevertheless, it is only one expression and for its own health it needs other sources of intimacy and socialization. A neighborhood, for example, should mean a group of friendly helpers who are neither part of the family nor alien forces.

Because of the peculiar history of the United States, forms of community other than the family have had difficulty surviving. The United States is a highly individualistic country built from immigrants always on the move. The one community that survived the trip across the ocean, the movement to the frontier, the suburban exodus, and the climb up the corporate bureaucracy was the family. As a result, the family is given the impossible burden of producing the human being. The burden falls disproportionately on the mother who cannot avoid having enormous psychological influence on the child and is then criticized for her overcontrol.

Because the family never lives up to expectations, a reaction against the family is always another strand of United States history. Having no language of community free from family, the disillusioned ones strike out against the family. Community becomes a name of an antifamily. The nineteenth and twentieth centuries have produced numerous experiments in utopian communities that would eliminate the family.[18] High ideals can be found next to brutal attitudes that run counter to natural human feelings. Religious sects often try to strip people of their past family association so that they can enter the community of the saved. Family does not die that easily, however, and utopian experiments often perpetuate familial roles in distorted form, especially when a powerful father figure has disciples dependent on him.

It would not be fair to dismiss all utopian experiments as sick or evil. Utopian communities have done many good things, but they are not a solution to the question of community for most people. Their danger is that they are a reverse side of the coin which collapses community into family. People in these experiments slip into speaking of themselves as living in community— instead of a family. If they take over the word "community" for themselves, they assign the other 99 percent to be without community.[19]

When the word "community" is identified with strange forms of antifamily, a counter action sets it. The defenders of the family become very suspicious of the word "community" but with the result that each isolated family is thrown back on its own resources. When Richard Nixon vetoed the child care bill in December 1971, he knew how to argue his case. The bill, Nixon said, "would commit the vast moral authority of the government to the side of communal approaches to child rearing over the family centered approach." The alternatives were traditionally American: family or community. With that choice any smart politician will be on the side of the family. But those who praise the family against community may not be the friends that the family needs. In a showdown between family and community, family will win, but it will be a pyrrhic victory. The family needs a context of non-familial but communal forms. Undeniably they do pose some threat to the family, but in the long run the health of the family is best served by the acknowledgment and development of other communal forms.

In this section I would like to identify by name some of these other expressions of community. I refer first to some general groupings which obviously exist though their impact is of questionable significance. I turn then to five specific forms whose existence raises fundamental questions about sex, marriage, and family.

There has always existed in the United States a host of "voluntary associations." Foreign commentators like Alexis de Tocqueville and Lord Bryce were impressed by the proliferation of these organizations in the United States.[20] Bowling clubs, civic clubs, theater parties, encounter groups, church suppers provide some experience of community. The neighborhood is also a reality in more than name in parts of the country, especially in ethnic enclaves of large cities and in small villages.[21]

I think it is permissible to extend the word "community" to these sometimes casual and often transitory groups. But I think the primary meaning of community has to refer to deeper forms of physical, psychological, and economic bonding. Non-familial communities need something comparable to the family's seriousness, depth, and permanence. There is danger in current talk of "having community" for a weekend or an hour a week. If community is the human process of growing toward unity/differences, then it involves the people one lives with, eats with, plays with, prays with, and shares risks with. People don't always do all of those things together, but community connotes a movement toward deep and lasting relationships.

I think it is possible to name five non-familial forms. Perhaps one could reduce the number or add a few more. But I would object to a kind of smorgasbord of "lifestyles" for people in quest of variety.[22] The five represent carefully structured forms which require care, discipline, and long-term stability. Literature which implies that human life is infinitely malleable is unrealistic. Programs that encourage people to experiment with all forms of sexual relation are anticommunal. The first two of the following forms overlap the family circle. The third and fourth overlap a meaning of marital but not of familial. The fifth is the most distinct from marriage and family though it also requires discipline and dedication.

1. Family Networks

I refer by family networks to any close cooperation between families. Groupings of families could be helpful to any family but would especially be helpful to those that are incomplete or "broken." There is no proof that one-parent families have a poorer record of crime or sickness, but they obviously carry a great burden in a society based on isolated family units.[23] Fifty percent of households headed by women are below the government's poverty level. Herbert Gutman has shown that the black family survived in ways that whites did not recognize.[24] Black families, broken or not, functioned in networks. Ironically, some whites are now discovering this principle of black survival.

One of the reasons for the discovery of family networks is economic pressure. Families may find that it is helpful to form some kind of economic collective. Against the modern corporation the individual family is helpless. Of itself the collective does not put the family back into the nucleus of economic power, but it does begin to break down walls of economic isolation.

The obvious and specific purpose of grouping families is child care. A family network *is* a child care center. Most mothers of small children now work outside the home. This fact need not be bad news; the involvement of the mother in her own work should be a help to the children. But the mother of a family in our society cannot simply add work time to her day. She needs cooperation not only from her husband but from other men and women. An issue like child abuse is not exclusively the concern of the isolated family nor can it be solved exclusively within that setting. The proper way to ask the question of child care today is: "If we as a human community want children, how does society propose to provide?"[25] Government involvement in this area is a mixed blessing. Local government could contribute in the form of tax credits. Whatever is done by government, nothing prevents three or four families from inventing their own child care center.[26]

2. Communes

A commune is a group of adults who function as a unit in a common household. Communes could include family units within the household. Children who are reared in a commune can have a rich upbringing. Urie Bronfenbrenner has said that every child needs some time with an adult who is "crazy about" him/her; at other times the child should spend time with adults who do not have that attitude.[27] Ideally, a commune might provide that environment. However, if a family is in a commune, the relation has to be carefully structured lest the children are neglected and exploited.[28]

A central problem of communes has always been sex. They usually try either to ban sex altogether or else to prescribe that it should be shared with all. Sexual pairing is what the commune finds disruptive. A commune in which sex is shared with everyone has yet to be proved a workable scheme. In contrast, the absence of sexual expression has been proved successful at least for some people at some times. As a discipline for the young or as a comfortable place for old people, the commune may be appropriate.

Communes, especially those which are restrictive of sex, need a religious aspect.[29] A vision of an ideal, a code of conduct, a discipline of life, and liturgical celebration have characterized successful communes. A religious discipline today would include a stand on housing, food, noise, drugs, and public utilities. It would also include a stand against sexual exploitation. A religious organization should have a place for those who by choice or necessity do not engage in sexual expression. But the religious organization should not collapse the word "community" to those who do not engage in sex. Any religious group should be concerned that the sexual expression in the lives of its members be sources of joy and holiness.

3. Homophile Relations

Sexual love between two persons of the same sex has difficulty getting recognized in this society and probably in most societies. In one of the most comprehensive books on "adult psychology" the only reference to homosexual love is: "For a small group of adults sexual deviancy from the social norm may eliminate their marrying the opposite sex. Homosexuality may be so powerfully felt that marriage may be avoided under any circumstances."[30] That is certainly short shrift for tens of millions of people in the United States.

Homophile love is a dramatic challenge to the ideal of the adult male as head of the family. Relations between men have usually been the main object of attack. The reason was that one of the men was seen to be lowering his dignity and acting like a woman. The frightening part was that he was revealing the passive or receptive element that may be in every man. Society's defense is to equate homosexuality with inversion.[31] Stereotypes and jokes assume that one person is playing the man and the other the woman despite the fact that this is not usually the case.

Whatever pathology may now surround homosexuality, the admission of the possibility of homophile relations is central to the second ideal of adulthood. More study and experience are needed before homosexuality can be better understood. What can be done immediately is that society stop persecuting people who are homosexually oriented. Eventually there may be a clearer social form for the support of homophile relationships. The persons partake of the meaning of marry but not the meaning of family. Since marriage has been a contract for establishing the family, its meaning cannot be easily separated from family. Thus, a legal marriage ceremony today would probably push a homosexual relation in the direction of family roles which is not what homosexual love is.

4. Married Singles

I am using here a paradoxical phrase to describe the lives of millions of people in the United States today. A married couple is part of an institution for the rearing of children. I take that institution to be good, necessary, and indestructible. But many men and women who love each other do not intend to have their own families. They wish to marry (deep and abiding sexual love) but not enter marriage (the contract for establishing the family). They need a new form which partakes of both married and single.[32]

Young people are the obvious group to whom this applies. If people continue to enter the ancient institution of marriage but stop having children, they may not feel that they have been liberated. In fact, they may feel more restricted than in the past unless other changes occur. For parents, especially the mother, children were a heavy responsibility but also a contact with the rest of life.

The problem of the young is also showing up in later middle age. Many older people are having difficulty adjusting to a long life after the children have left.[33] What men and women need are personal and professional involvements that might be lessened during the child-rearing years. For men and women without families or for men and women whose families are grown up, the trappings of family life may not make much sense. Elements like the traditional marriage contract, the one-family home, the one-family car, and the woman as "housewife" can become a burden upon the love and productivity of their lives.

5. Communal Singles

There are, finally, people who seem to lead full human lives without the existence of one special person or a commune. Often they draw their sustenance from a lively urban center and are involved with politics, education, or the arts. The number of one-person households has been climbing sharply in the last decade. Some of these adults are in temporary transition between marriages. Others are in the groups I described as married single or homophile. Still other people are working out their lives as individuals related to the communities about them.

In the seventeenth century a man was not allowed to live alone. If he could not start his own household, he had to present himself to the town selectmen and be assigned to a family. Such laws existed in Plymouth, Massachusetts Bay, Connecticut, and Virginia.[34] Pressure was brought upon an adult to marry and then to "cohabit in harmony." Young people who wish to challenge the restrictiveness of the past ought to challenge the meaning of "to live with." Must one occupy a common household to be a responsible adult? Someone in a single-person household could have a strong communal life if he or she finds ways of living with, working with, and loving other people. The lives of communal single people need a shape or form which is difficult to attain but is apparently now necessary for society.

From the preceding material I would like to draw three conclusions for Protestant and Catholic churches.

1. A parish or local church is probably not a community. This conclusion is worded negatively, but it is not meant as an attack upon church or parish. Instead of using the word "community" to refer unrealistically to itself, the parish could try to help the communal expression where it is in people's lives. The parish can function as the large organization which supports community. Large organization is indispensable in today's world. The important question is whether the basic unit of large organization is either the individual/family in isolation or else groups, including families, in interaction.

Size is always an issue in questions of community. A small number of people does not guarantee the existence of a community, but a large number of people usually precludes it. Catholic parishes in and near large cities often have thousands of people. The recognition that the parish is not a community often leads to the proposal to split the parish. The proposal misunderstands the problem. Dividing 1500 families into two groups of 750 is almost certainly going in the wrong direction.

The better route is to let the parish be the orgnizational umbrella under which many communal groups can be formed. The number of people that can be a community is not arbitrary. There is an upper limit for the number of individuals who can interact with intimacy, mutuality, and personal care. Thus, even parishes with a hundred people are far too large to be a community, but they can be a great help to the community experience of people's lives.

2. Churches should be places for the meeting of familial and non-familial forms. The Catholic practice of describing a parish by the number of its families is misleading. The Protestant practice of counting individual adults is not satisfactory, either. If the parish appears to be well described by a figure for families, then the parish's location may not be typical of the national population. A more likely explanation is that the parish by its pattern of self-description simply eliminates all the people who do not fit its family category. Does parish language reflect the great number of widows or divorced people in our midst? Do programs exclude older people by reason of time, place, or physical setting?

There may be a need for some alienated groups to have their own organization. That does not mean each parish needs to have a widows' club. But some groups such as homosexuals and divorced people may need special transitional organization. The purpose of "Dignity" is not to set up a homosexual church but to provide support for homosexual people.[35] The eventual aim should be communities that cut across these divisions. If the parish is not ready to embrace all differences, it could still open communication in an educational setting.

3. The church/parish should give concrete support to family life. Parenthood has not been getting a good press in recent years. The church should be in the forefront of opposition to this inhuman attitude. The care of children is an ultimate test for any community. A diversity which the church can supply to children is the presence of adults, especially older adults. The church can also help parents with specific skills for their jobs.

Church educators should be cautious about saying that religious education is the responsibility of the family. Sidney Callahan puts the issue cryptically: "The first mission of the church in family religious education is to transcend the family."[36] The other parts of the schooling-laboratory model of education should be available to the family. We could use less rhetoric from church officials on the parent as primary religious educator. What parents do need is a communal setting and the chance to acquire skills that will help them to exercise their responsibility with confidence.

Notes

1. For the difference between this principle as an ideal and the actual situation in the seventeenth and eighteenth centuries, see William Chafe, *Women and Equality: Changing Patterns in American Culture* (New York, Oxford, 1977), p. 21.

2. See Mary Cable, *The Little Darlings* (New York, Scribner, 1975).

3. See Robert Jewett and John Lawrence, *The American Monomyth* (Garden City, Doubleday, 1977), p. 116.

4. See Erik Erikson, *Childhood and Society*, 2nd ed. (New York, Norton, 1963), pp. 285–325.

5. Catherine Beecher, *A Treatise in Domestic Economy for the Use of Young Ladies at Home and at School* (Boston, Marsh, Capen, Lyon, Webb, 1841).

6. Alice Rossi, "A Biosocial Perspective on Parenting," *Daedalus*, 106(Spring, 1977), p. 14.

7. Philippe Ariès, "The Family and the City," *Daedalus*, 106(Spring, 1977), pp. 227–35.

8. See Fred Hirsch, *Social Limits to Growth* (Cambridge, Harvard, 1976).

9. William Bradford, *History of Plymouth Plantation*, ed. Samuel Morison (New York, Modern Library, 1952), p. 334.

10. For a typical exchange of this kind, see William O'Neill and Urie Bronfenbrenner in *Psychology Today*, August, 1977, pp. 10f.

11. John Demos, *A Little Commonwealth: Family Life in the Plymouth Colony* (New York, Oxford, 1970); see also Kenneth Lockridge, *A New England Town: The First 100 Years* (New York, Norton, 1970): Peter Laslett, *The World We Have Lost* (New York, Scribner, 1965).

12. See Arlie Hochschild, *The Unexpected Community* (Englewood Cliffs, Prentice-Hall, 1973).

13. For a discussion of the family's need to be strengthened against the intrusions of state and professionalism, see Christopher Lasch, *Haven in a Heartless World* (New York, Basic, 1977), pp. 134–89.

14. See L. S. Stavrianos, *The Promise of the Coming Dark Age* (San Francisco, Freeman, 1976), p. 28.

15. See Bernice Lott, "Who Wants the Children?" in *Intimacy, Family and Society*, ed. Arlene Skolnick and Jerome Skolnick (Boston, Little, Brown and Co., 1974), pp. 390–406.

16. See Emory Elliot, *Power and the Pulpit in Puritan New England* (Princeton, Princeton University, 1975); Perry Miller, *Errand into the Wilderness* (New York, Harper, 1956), pp. 1–15.

17. See Roberto Unger, *Knowledge and Politics* (New York, Free Press, 1975), p. 220.

18 See Rosabeth Moss Kanter, *Commitment and Community* (Cambridge, Harvard, 1972); Russel Jacoby, *Social Amnesia* (Boston, Beacon, 1975).

19. Note the practice of the Roman Catholic Church which regularly uses the term "religious community" as a description of the less than 1 percent of its members who are in religious orders/congregations.

20. See Nisbet, *op. cit.*, p. 273.

21. See Lewis Mumford. *The Transformations of Man* (New York, Collier, 1962), p. 146.

22. As an example of this kind of writing, see Ronald Mazur, *The New Intimacy* (Boston, Beacon, 1973).

23. Joyce Ladner, *Tomorrow's Tomorrow: The Black Woman* (Garden City, Doubleday, 1971); Carol Stack, *All Our Kin* (New York, Harper and Row, 1974).

24. Herbert Gutman, *The Black Family in Slavery and Freedom 1750–1925* (New York, Pantheon, 1975).

25. Jean Baker Miller, *Toward a New Psychology of Women* (Boston, Beacon, 1976), p. 128.

26. On local experiments, see Wanda Burgess, "Learning to Cooperate: A Middle Class Experiment," in *The Future of the Family*, ed. Louise Kapp Howe (New York, Touchstone, 1972); on government's involvement and cost. see Meredith Larson, *Federal Policy for Preschool Services* (Menlo Park, Stanford Research Institute, 1975), pp. 19–20.

27. Urie Bronfenbrenner, "The American Family in Trouble," *Psychology Today*, May, 1977, p. 43; Christel Bookhagen, "Kommune 2: Childrearing in the Commune," in *Family, Marriage and the Struggle of the Sexes*, ed. Hans Peter Dreitzel (New York, Macmillan, 1972), pp. 138–75.

28. See John Rothchild and Susan Berns, *The Children of the Counterculture* (Garden City, Doubleday, 1976).

29. See Kanter, *op. cit.*, pp. 136–38: Douglas Sturm, "The Kibbutzim and the Spirit of Israel: An Interpretive Essay," in *The Family, Communes and Society,* ed. Sallie Teselle (New York, Harper Torchbook, 1972), pp. 116–18.

39. Leonard Bischof, *Adult Psychology,* 2nd ed. (New York, Harper and Row, 1976), p. 274.

31. See C. A. Tripp, *The Homosexual Matrix* (New York, Signet, 1976), pp. 20ff.

32. A similar point is made by Margaret Mead in "Marriage in Two Steps," in *The Family in Search of a Future*, ed. Herbert Otto (New York, Appleton-Century-Crofts, 1970), pp. 75–84.

33. On the "empty nest syndrome" in the nineteenth and twentieth centuries, see "Demographic Change and the Life Cycle of American Families," in *The Family in History*, ed. Theodore Rabb and Robert Rotberg (New York, Harper & Row, 1971).

34. See Morgan, *op. cit.*, p. 145; Clinton Rossiter, *The First American Revolution* (New York, Harcourt, Brace and World, 1956), p. 151.

35. John McNeill, *The Church and the Homosexual* (Kansas City, Sheed Andrews and McMeel, 1976), p. 186.

36. Sidney Callahan, "Family Religious Education," *Living Light*, 11(Summer, 1974), p. 260.

6. Forms of Learning

I wish to look in this chapter at the forms that learning takes as one progresses into adulthood. If the analysis of the previous five chapters has been accurate, many of the elements will reappear here. Thus, this chapter should serve to recapitulate what has already been presented while adding some details about ages and stages of adult learning.

A common theme in adult education literature is that adults learn from a "problem-centered" approach whereas children learn subjects or disciplines. This claim is misleading. What is really being contrasted is not adult and child but rather schooling and laboratory modes of learning. Schooling is for systematic study in a curriculum. Laboratory (work-retreat-family/community) is centered on "problems of life." The schooling/laboratory mix should change throughout life, but one should resist the tendency to assign school to children and life problems to adults.

Why is it so constantly repeated that adult learning is "problem-centered"? The reason comes from what I have referred to as the first ideal of adulthood, namely, the rational, autonomous, economically productive individual. This literature assumes that when one is a child and radically dependent, learning is defined by someone else. When one becomes an adult, one's position is reversed. The adult is self-directing and chooses to learn only what is personally interesting. Just as one legally passes a line from being a child to being an adult, so a learner also passes a line and henceforth learns as an adult.

105

This adult education language is not as revolutionary as it sees itself. Stereotypes about children are reinforced while adults are lumped together and assigned a way of learning that is the opposite of the child's. The adult's way of learning turns out to be individualistic, rationalistic, and anti-institutional. Some social groups do not fit well into this stereotype of "how an adult learns." Old people tend to disappear from the discussion and differences between men and women do not show up.

Adult education over many decades established its own terrain by opposing adult and child. However, there is now a rapidly growing body of literature that actually describes stages and phases of adulthood. This new material does not fit into a simplistic opposition of child and adult. There are writers who are still attacking people for not opposing adult learner and child learner, but that has ceased to be the question. Perhaps there are people somewhere who think there are no differences between adults and children, but it would be difficult to find them. However, people who reject child vs. adult as a language are not equating child and adult. On the contrary, they are looking for the great variety and complexity both in the lives of children and in the lives of adults.

This new body of literature which comes from a combination of disciplines helps to describe the second ideal of adulthood. In this case, adulthood is what people grow into all of their lives, each in his or her unique way. We need to describe learning in a way that shows the continuity of development from birth to death but also allows for proper emphases and differences throughout the life span. It is never simply a question of identifying adult learning rather than child learning. For example, a person's sense of time varies greatly if one is 5, 12, 40, or 70 years old. Overlapping those ages, time is experienced differently for men and women. Furthermore, a 35-year-old career woman and a 35-year-old mother at home experience time differently.

This chapter is organized in the following way: 1) I will note what effect the first ideal of adulthood has on adult learning; 2) I will recount the adjustments introduced into that picture by some twentieth-century studies of adults; 3) I will describe the more radical redesign of learning and development in what is called "life-span literature"; 4) I will propose ways that organizations, including churches, might respond to this new material.

Similar to the picture of the family in Chapter Five, the concept and the study of learning reflect society's commitment to the first ideal of adulthood. That ideal presumes that we are to traverse childhood in a series of learning tasks so as to fit into the world of the adult.

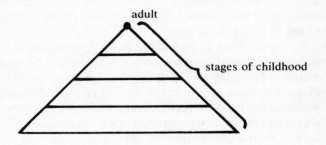

[1a]

The perfect adult would have learned to form his or her own ideas, principles, and decisions. Most adults (in the biological sense) do not seem to become adult (in the sense of ideal). That peculiar disjunction between biological fact and psychosocial ideal should give us pause. Perhaps it is a tragedy of the human race that so many people don't grow up or perhaps the problem is an educational lag which can be overcome by greater effort. However, I think the question has to be raised whether the ideal itself is the most preferable one.

If society conceives of learning according to the above diagram, then the study of learning and the study of children's learning become almost identical. A field called "developmental psychology" developed from child psychology. No one would deny that the study of the child's learning development is important and useful. But an exclusive attention to children not only overlooks much of human development, but can even distort the meaning of learning in children. The aspects of development that get emphasized tend to be mechanical and psychometric tasks of learning.

Some of the most brilliant work on children's development has been done by Jean Piaget. Anyone working with children cannot neglect Piaget's findings on stages of development that he names "cognitive." He distinguishes four main stages as sensory-motor, pre-operational, concrete operational, and formal operational. A child progresses through these stages in a definite way. The development is biologically based, unidirectional, necessary, and irreversible. The stages describe an increasing ability to use abstract reasoning.[1]

Piaget's work is invaluable for designing school curricula for children. There is no sense trying to teach a child laws of mathematics which are of necessity incomprehensible to the child. Piaget's work is helpful in the area of religion. Sensitive teachers of the young have probably always known that a Bible story for a 6-year-old is more appropriate than a catechism definition. Concern with the psychology of the child leads to a more patient approach to teaching and to less material in the curriculum.

The great strength of Piaget's work is also its limitation. Piaget undoubtedly recognizes the limits of his findings. That fact doesn't prevent his work being used in a way that implies that human development is mainly a question of cognitive development in children. The problem becomes more apparent when the Piagetan scheme is transposed to other areas of social, moral, or religious development.

A scheme of "moral development" described by Lawrence Kohlberg has been influential in recent years. The severe limitations of this scheme get overlooked as people make generalizations about moral development. Kohlberg acknowledges that he is only studying the moral reasoning of his subjects or rather the capacity to form certain judgments classified as moral. The connection between such reasoning and moral behavior remains highly mysterious. Kohlberg has searched for a "stage" outside his scheme of six stages that might explain people moving through stages.[2]

What is apparent in Kohlberg's scheme is an ideal of moving to more rational, individual, and abstract modes of reasoning. Although that direction may be desirable and even inevitable in the cognitive development of a child, the use of this kind of sequence for morality and for adults may obscure as much as it reveals. My suspicion is supported by the claim made that most adults don't get to the top part of the scheme. An inevitable air of condescension comes in here. Those who understand and apply the theory are presumably among the few who are morally well developed. Those who are being classified tend to fail the system and not get beyond the fourth rung.

There is an alternate explanation, namely, that this scheme doesn't help much in describing the moral lives of the adult population. People may be behaving morally but not in ways that register on a scale of moral reasoning. There may be forms of social learning and human activity for which individualistic and rationalistic questions are hardly relevant.[3] It could be asked, for example, whether a word like "cognitive" makes sense outside that narrowly defined path in children's lives which Piaget describes. At the least I think we should be extremely cautious about judgments on "moral development" until we are sure that the human race has such a scheme.

In this section I would like to describe what I call "adjustments" in the picture of learning described above. The basis of the picture was the study of children. In the last half-century adults have been studied as well as children and the findings were attached to what was known of children. A sizable body of material has now been amassed on the learning abilities of adults and the obstacles to adult learning.

The beginning point for this part of the story is a book by E. L. Thorndike, *Adult Learning* (1928).[4] Thorndike's study is rather clearly connected to the experimental psychology that preceded his study of the adult. The intelligence quotient had been developed in the first quarter of the century with a scale that used 16 years old as the normal level and 18 years old as superior. The assumption was that the ability to learn reaches a peak at the end of childhood and then declines. Obviously, people continue to learn things, but it was thought that their ability to learn decreased. Geniuses in history who seemed to contradict the principle were thought to be simply exceptions to the rule.

Thorndike's study challenged this assumption that adults

lose the ability to learn. Judged by today's standards, Thorndike may seem like a reactionary. The amusing thing is that he was the liberal of his day when it came to adult learning. One of his main conclusions is that a person between 25 and 40 should not be afraid to plunge into study and learning. Up to age 45 there is a decline in learning ability (1 percent per year after 25), but one's ability to learn is not seriously impaired. What Thorndike was doing was raising the ceiling from 25 to 45 before the serious and inevitable decline set in. Thus, we have a slight adjustment in the first diagram.

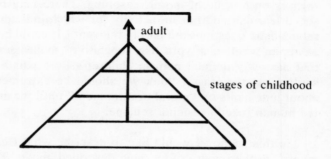

[1b]

The contemporary reader is not likely to be satisfied with this modestly liberal conclusion. Of course, the issue is not one to be solved by opinion, bias, or vague hope. On the other hand, neither is the issue resolvable by a set of scientific experiments that will produce indisputable data for correlating age and ability. Do intelligence, learning, or "cognitive performance" decline with age? The answer depends in large part on how these words are defined. For example, Thorndike included speed of response as an element within his test of learning. The supposition that speed is a valid criterion of intelligence is debatable; most researchers today would probably exclude it.

More difficult to manage are all the other variables in people's makeup besides age. Methods have been devised to factor out those elements (educational background, experience with tests, sex, social position), but a complete elimination is probably impossible. Most important is the question whether intelligence and learning ability are accurately judged by the mechanical tests and measurable bits of learning found in these studies. Even the most sophisticated forms of IQ test seem increasingly irrelevant as people get older.

Despite this criticism and the need for reserve about these studies, some important conclusions have been reached. The most important generalization to be made is: There is no proof that intelligence and the ability to learn ever have to decline in one's life.[5] Several qualifications have to be attached to this conclusion. Accidents and disabilities do occur in people's lives. Furthermore, the principle is stated negatively: There is no proof that ability must decline. Even granting these restrictions, this principle is a large and encouraging step for the human race. The principle represents a major turn in the rationalistic ideal that has dominated Western society.

Further precision in regard to this principle includes the following three points:

1. Most of the studies of learning ability have been done with people of higher-than-average ability. Reaching a true cross section of the population is very difficult. However, no great differences in the learning curve have so far been discovered on the basis of high or low ability.

2. What has been clearly shown is that some things can interfere with learning as one gets older. The two most important obstacles are disuse and disease. Learning is not like an empty jar: The more you put in it the less room remains. On the contrary, the more one learns the more one can learn. Nothing helps school learning so much as having continued one's schooling. Nothing obstructs learning so much as long intervals when learning has been neglected.

Injury to part of the body obviously can interfere with learning or specific kinds of learning. Age eventually causes decay, but if the body is taken care of, that need not happen until the 70s, 80s, or beyond. Even then some compensations can be introduced. A large part of the population wears eyeglasses because the eyes have been subjected to extraordinary strains. The same may soon be true of hearing which is second in importance to sight for affecting learning ability as one gets older.[6] The lesson here is clear: Individuals and society have to take care of health so that organic diseases do not become an insuperable obstacle to long and fruitful lives.

3. There is a need to distinguish kinds of learning and intelligence. For example, as one gets older, the memory changes. One doesn't lose the power to remember, but the method of retaining and retrieving material changes. Few people as they get older have the kind of recall often found in young people. Nonetheless, the re-creating and synthesizing possible in adulthood may make the memory more effective for life situations. This point on memory leads to attempts to distinguish kinds of intelligence. Some elements within intelligence may go up, others go down. A single measurement may miss both movements. R. B. Cattell and John Horn refer to crystallized intelligence (e.g., much verbal knowledge) and fluid intelligence (e.g., the memory recall of a child). Crystallized refers to abilities that are supported by institutions of acculturation while fluid abilities are not. As might be expected, Horn finds that crystallized intelligence tends to stay even or go up while fluid intelligence decreases with time.[7]

The experimental work described above developed as an extension of laboratory work with children and animals. The emphasis is psychological and the product is numerical descriptions concerning the ability to perform measurable tasks. What has been learned about adulthood this way is important but restricted. Another body of literature has also grown up over the last half century. Sometimes this second body of material overlaps the first, but its orientation is more social and humanistic, deriving its data from biographies of men and women. The result of this work could be a quite revolutionary change of outlook on the ages and stages of the human being. Instead of "raising the ceiling of learning," this approach might rethink childhood and youth in light of their being steps along the way to adulthood.

The beginning of interest in this approach is difficult to assign. Artists, like Shakespeare, have through the centuries spoken of the "ages of man." The start of twentieth-century systematic interest should perhaps be credited to G. Stanley Hall. Hall is best known for his classic on adolescence in 1904, but toward the end of his life he wrote *Senescence: The Last Half of Life*. In that book Hall turned upside down the assumption about deterioration in old age: "There is a certain maturity of judgment about men, things, causes and life generally, that nothing in the world but years can bring, a real wisdom that only age can teach."[8]

Major credit in this area is usually given to Erik Erikson who in 1950 described a life cycle of eight stages.[9] The three stages for adults were named *intimacy* (vs. isolation), *generativity* (vs. stagnation), and *integrity* (vs. despair). Erikson had much more to say of children than he did of adults. He admitted that we are still only on the threshold of the age of the adult. Many people are now trying to expand on Erikson's brief suggestions. Much of the work is speculative though there are some controlled studies of life-span development. The methodological problems here are enormous and while improvements will undoubtedly be made in coming decades, the nature of the question may make some problems insoluble.

Two problems of method should be immediately noted.

1. The Relation of Age and Cohort

There is always a question of whether people are the way they are because of the age they are or because of the generation in which they were born. Are sexual attitudes of 45-year-old people today reflective of their age or their having lived through the last four decades of history? The best way to handle this question is to use longitudinal rather than cross-sectional samples, that is, to follow groups through their lifetime rather than study several age groupings of people today. Of course, longitudinal studies of adult life are the most difficult samples possible. It may take most of a century to collect the data during which time the researcher changes and eventually dies. Fortunately, several studies were started in the 1920s and 1930s so that some data are available now.[10]

2. Sex and Other Variables

Although men and women go through much the same sequence in life, they are seldom at the same place at the same time. Life-span commentators must regularly introduce qualifying statements about sex. Not surprisingly, women are underrepresented in most longitudinal studies started long ago. These studies also underrepresent lower economic classes and minority groups in the United States. For studying adult development, race, religion, and privilege are important factors but ones not fully integrated in studies up to this time.

The study of adult development emerged from studies of old age at one end and adolescence at the other. Then an interest developed in the "midlife crisis," perhaps because it bore striking resemblance to adolescence. What is now being attempted is a filling out of the periods before and after the midlife crisis. The scheme is still sketchy, but a number of authors have added flesh to Erikson's suggestions. There are exceptions to the pattern and some important distinctions, but the general pattern is the following:[11]

1. A period of leaving home ("All I know is I want out")
2. The 20s with strong differences among men, career women, and women nurturing a family
3. A transitional point near 30
4. A settling down in the 30s
5. A major change in outlook between 35–45, generally coming earlier for women
6. A calmer period in the 50s
7. A changed outlook with old age, especially if one retires from work

What strikes me about the main transitional points is that they all involve a spiritual or religious crisis. Adolescence first came to be defined and described as the time of religious conversion. Although the nineteenth century distorted the connection between age and conversion, the twentieth-century adolescent still asks "Who am I?" and "What's the meaning of life?" Conversion to religion may often supply adolescents with premature answers to these questions, but if society wishes to lessen the influence of destructive sects, it has to supply a better setting in which adolescents can live with and work at religious questions.[12]

Old age is also a deeply religious time in life. For many if not all people, the imminence of death raises questions of the ultimate meaning of life. Studies of religiosity which concentrate on certain behavior (e.g., church attendance) may not capture the religious intensity of old age. If a society is trying to forget about old age and death, it may not recognize the religious issue which comes from the old.[13]

The transition of midlife seems to be a reawakening of the adolescent question about life and a first awareness of old age's question about death. The 40-year-old is like the 16-year-old in trying to decide what life means, but the second time around the question may be more painful: "What he is involved in is not so much a quest for identity as an inquest."[14] The fourth transitional point around the age of 30 is not as clear-cut as the other three. However, to the extent that it is reported, especially among men, it carries echoes of the same religious question: How can I find a renewed commitment that will make my life meaningful and successful?

It seems to me that religious issues remain to be explored much more fully than they have. Religion tends to get identified with certain ecclesiastical forms and is then interpreted in mainly negative terms. In Gail Sheehy's *Passages* religion seldom appears and then only as something to be freed from.[15] Modern researchers may not have tools adequate to the study of religion and the adults studied tend to exclude racial and ethnic groups in which religion is important. Elisabeth Kubler-Ross's experience is pertinent here. She had no special interest in religion when she began working with dying patients. She still finds inculcated dogmas a hindrance more than a help to the dying. But she has also discovered a level of religious attitudes, symbols, and convictions that are part of a reconciliation with death.[16]

I would like to summarize data on adult development by using the educational model described in Chapter Three. I shall use the laboratory part of my model to give focus to the data now available on adult learning. Later in the chapter I will come back to schooling.

1. Family/Community

People learn by caring for and loving each other. Spouses and parents learn in a way and to a degree that psychological experiments can never fully capture.[17] The very concept one has of learning is affected by whether one's parents are strong persons in the foreground or weak persons in the background. Being a parent to a small child and a parent of an adolescent create very different attitudes to learning and to self.

The 20s are for most people a time of love and development of what Erikson called "intimacy." The majority of people marry in their 20s and the bloom remains for at least some years. For men the 20s are also a time of career plans and a "dream" of success. Men's lives seem dominated by a loved partner and a "mentor" in the area of work. For most women the period has been one of creating the home and starting a family. Despite the prevalence of this situation few works describe the young wife and mother from inside those roles. The typical child care manual has been written by a doctor, usually older and nearly always male. Parenthood as a developmental phase, especially as described by a mother at home with small children, remains almost unreported.[18]

Women who chose careers and have been successful at them go through a different pattern than the (current) majority of women. An intriguing study of their lives has been done by Margaret Hennig and Anne Jardim.[19] The twenty-five women in this study received unusual support from their fathers, remained loyal to one company, and were brought up short by personal questions at age 35. They had chosen career before family, but they rediscovered love after achieving success at work. The age of 35 is apparently quite precise in a woman's life because of biology. Women who have not had careers also found a different impulse in their lives at about this age. Looking ahead, many women begin to wonder what they will do after the children are grown.

Men can postpone the questioning, but when they come to it, the crash is harder. Forty-year-old men in our society seem squeezed from every direction. They may have difficult relations with aging parents, with their children to whom they feel some resentment, and with their spouses who are at a different stage of personal development. Whereas at 30 the man may have a great dream and the woman may be bored, age 40 often reverses their positions.

There is no solution for marital conflict at 40 except to know that a few years more will help to heal much of the discord. Couples who stay together often find considerable help from each other in later years. That development, however, requires some outlet for the woman's energies and some refashioning of the man's dreams.

Old age could be a rich time for teaching and learning. Unfortunately, it is an age not well appreciated or understood in our society. To be a grandparent, for example, is a stage of learning development. For those who are not grandparents it should be possible to become a "foster grandparent." The young as well as the old would profit from intergenerational exchange. Old age, to be fruitful, has to include contact with children and youth as well as with one's adult children. Friends, even if there are few of them, become very important in old age.[20]

2. Work

Studies of the life span show that work is a central issue of adult development. There are variations according to sex and age, but everyone needs work. Education ought to resist identifying work with the job a man does until he "retires." Women need significant work to do and both men and women need some kind of activity in their old age.

Work of a productive and mastering kind is important to most men in their 20s and 30s. Women whose work is mainly in the home with children are often not recognized as working. What is not paid for does not get classified as work even though it may be

an indispensable contribution to society. Educators ought to lead
the way in describing work so that it includes those tens of millions of women.

A remarkable change occurs for most women and men in the
course of their work. Women begin looking for another kind of
work that would tap technical skills and aggressive attitudes. Men
are brought up short (often by their first heart attack) and begin
questioning the value of all their hard work. The stark contrast of
men and women may be finding special expression in the 1970s:
The 40-year-old man is bored by his work and feels as if life is
almost over, while the 40-year-old woman is excited about career
possibilities stretching for decades of life before her.

What may seem to be a further cruel twist for men is that
earlier success does not make the midlife crisis any easier. If
anything, hard work and success make the crisis worse. A revealing study in this area is Elliott Jaques's "Death and the Midlife
Crisis."[21] Jaques found that men of special talent underwent a
severe crisis in their late 30s. Among geniuses he studied, the
death rate during the years 35–39 took an enormous jump.
Jaques's clinical work has confirmed his historical studies and
other writers note the same phenomenon: Success breeds crisis.[22]
What does one do for a second act if the first one has been
especially good? Men in their 20s who throw themselves totally
into their work are in danger of becoming 35-year-old burnouts.

Men in their 40s need either a new career or a new hold on
their old career. Where men simply resign themselves to go on in
the same old way and wait for retirement, middle age is not a very
pleasant time of life. Where men do refashion their dreams, they
eventually join women in new forms of work. As a common characteristic of this period, Bernice Neugarten finds a move from
active to passive mastery of environment.[23] The professional
athlete probably needs a new job, the policeman may need a new
form of police work. Men and women at this age might helpfully
redesign society's work so that it wouldn't harm the young adult
or exclude the old adult.

If middle-aged adults have successfully adjusted their skills,
they shouldn't ever have to retire from work. A retirement age for
a specific job may be useful or necessary. But people should not

have to stop working, that is, contributing productively to the well-being of the world. Maggie Kuhn, founder of the Gray Panthers, was challenged on her statement that she would work until her death. She was asked: Don't you mean "until you are physically not able to do it, which may be long before you die"? Her answer was: "People without health and vigor can be an important part of the radical critique of our society, that their very weakness can be a strength."[24] The old have something to teach the young by demonstrating what work really means and how one can work even with handicaps.

3. Retreat

The other side of the work coin is retreat. Forced retreat, especially for women and the old, is not desirable, but what has been preserved in quiet spots of the world should not be lost in movements of liberation. Men eventually come to find retreat in one way or another; unfortunately it is often by illness from overwork. Hennig found in her study of career women a time of moratorium at age 35. These women did not stop working, but for a year or two they got some distance from their work and let other sides of their personalities flower.

A lack of attention to the retreat element is probably related to the underdeveloped way religion is seen in the life span. Retreat does not belong exclusively to religion, but a religious education should certainly include zones of quiet for meditation, reflection, and re-creation. Horace Bushnell, one of the great Christian writers of the nineteenth century, was among the first to write on stages of development. He was also specially attentive to leisure or retreat as an element in religious education. "Never be in a hurry to believe; never try to conquer doubts against time. Time is one of the great elements in thought as truly as in motion."[25]

As one passes from middle age to old age a natural process of interiorization occurs. A certain amount of detachment from career and work is quite common. Quiet moments with a spouse, a friend, or one's grown children take on new value. Through

much of a man's early adult life, work is what promises im-
mortality. Some men may hold on to that illusion for their whole
lives, but a midlife change brings many men to their senses. When
one's parents die and when the obituary page becomes a regular
part of one's reading, the fragility of a career becomes an experienced fact. One may then be ready for the discovery that "the
imperishable intuitions come only to a man during his moments of
leisure" (Josef Pieper). Experimental psychology here again is
not very effective in measuring this kind of learning, but peace
and quiet can be great teachers.

Although the material outlined in this chapter is sketchy, a
few conclusions can be drawn for institutions which supply
schooling and other educational services. I will first discuss universities, community colleges, and other agencies that should be
providing schooling throughout a person's whole life. Then I will
look at the Catholic Church's sacramental system as an example
of what could be life-span religious development.

1. Schooling: The University

I began this chapter by referring to a misleading principle in
adult education literature. The statement is constantly reiterated
that adults want problem solving rather than subjects and disciplines. Unfortunately, universities have been very willing to operate by this principle. For most of the adult population the universities have offered a smorgasbord of problem-centered workshops and brief courses. The university may think it has thereby
fulfilled its responsibilities by providing "continuing education"
and "extension courses."

The worst thing about assuming that adults want to concentrate on problem solving is that the economic and social structure
will never change this way. The rich and the upper middle class
receive help in adjusting to their positions in life. The poor
without any systematic knowledge and training stay poor. Minority groups get very little leverage for political change.

The university's real job is to offer university training to everybody in the population, whatever their age. Not all adults want credit courses and degrees, but there is nonetheless an enormous market waiting for universities. Adults of any age are capable of earning university degrees and where there is realistic access to programs, adults do take the opportunity. What is still lacking is a change of attitude in many universities. Adult women remain a major source for the university to tap. Even in the 1970s, 90 percent of women between 30 and 45 years old did not have a college degree. At the same time one-half of the population over 65 did not have a ninth-grade education.

The findings discussed in this chapter would imply some relatively minor changes in universities to help adult learning. For example, lecture halls ought to be usable by people even if they have some disabilities of sight, hearing, or movement. Examinations ought not to put a premium on speed or certain kinds of memorization. The biggest difficulty for many adults is the first shock of the university. Libraries, administration buildings, and procedures with which they are unfamiliar can be intimidating; so can the (current) age of the student body. Many adults more than hold their own once they get through an initial period of adjustment which may be difficult. University staffs have to be sensitive to this brief but crucial problem.

2. Schooling: Community Colleges and Other Forms

Besides the more academic and literate training of the university, adults also need other kinds of learning. The community college has been a partial response to the need. If we truly get a community-based college, it should offer job retraining, preparation for leisure, family understanding, and self-help. A community college should be forming natural alliances with vocational schools, industry, government services, churches, and civic clubs. The learning in this setting is more of a problem-centered approach than in the university. Nevertheless, I am still talking about a systematic, disciplined, extensive course of study. A workshop that prepares someone to take an ocean cruise can have its place, but we also need long-term study on the place of leisure in life. There is a place for counseling cases of wife battering, but there is also need for extended analysis and reflection concerning midlife problems.

Churches can be one of the associates of community colleges. A church can offer a regular format of courses and workshops to help people in their understanding of religion. The first thing a church/parish has to be convinced of is the need to be committed to adult students on a permanent, continuous, and serious basis. Many churches will offer a four-week series in the fall and then decide, on the basis of how many people show up, whether to offer something further, perhaps a six-week course in Lent. What churches do not seem to realize is that no one would go to colleges if they operated on such a policy. Programs have to be operated around the year; they have to be organized in sequence and offer some variety. A church/parish that makes such a commitment will almost certainly find interested people.

Only a small percentage of a church/parish will ever attend such systematic study of the Bible, church history, church doctrine, or contemporary social problems. That is simply a fact of life which should be factored into decisions about the money and the extensiveness of the program. Small numbers do not mean that the program is unnecessary or undesirable. People running programs could become discouraged if they begin by assuming that everyone in the church/parish should be taking a course.

In my experience there is a more subtle discouragement which can occur for people running church educational programs. The study of adult development might obviate the problem. I refer to the fact that some people are great supporters of the courses for six months, a year, or two years; then they disappear. One need not assume that the church program failed. On the contrary, the course or program may have helped the person through a certain stage in life. The courses have to be continuously available, but not everyone will make continuous use of them.

The churches should not be trying simply to correlate religious answers and developmental stages for adults. Religious organizations are tempted to go after people in their weakest moments and so they search out the crisis points of development.

While the presence of religious help in crises is not to be disparaged, courses of study have a different purpose. Courses on the Bible or spirituality should be addressed to men and women in their strengths. That is, courses ought to be challenging the meaning of success in the lives of the successful. Courses ought to remind the hard-working that there is a need for retreat. Religious groups should be drawing from their own pasts a bigger picture that includes fantasy as well as technical reason, death as well as life. The Jewish and Christian Bibles remain an excellent source of study. Many Protestant churches already have firmly established Bible study for adults. These programs often just need a wider context and a livelier approach to the material.

For developing more stable and respectable courses of study, churches need to form working relationships with universities, seminaries, and community colleges. In those places today there are many well-trained and underemployed teachers. Some of them would enjoy teaching a course under church/parish auspices. Churches have a high degree of social acceptability, but it is not being used in attracting adult students. The biggest problem seems to be a timidity in breaking through ecclesiastical trappings and simply offering intelligent courses on religion to which everyone is welcome.

3. Sacraments

In this last section I would like to speculate on possible connections between the study of adult development and the sacramental system of the Catholic Church. Even as it now exists the sacramental system is a beautiful testimony to the life span. A person meets the rites of the Church on entry to life and after several important steps along the way is ushered from life with the oils for the sick. We now have more knowledge about stages of adulthood. We also have a better historical and conceptual understanding of sacraments.[26] The time may be ripe for beginning to rethink sacraments in a more radical way than in the past. We perhaps need a stage theory of sacraments in which one grows by degrees into marriage, orders, or reconciliation. An expansion and development of rites would not have to do violence to tradition, but the Catholic Church has to be bold about confronting the present. The following points are hints in that direction.[27]

A. *Matrimony*

We have a scarcity of symbols for affirming personal commitments. Young people need ways to formalize courtship or to experiment in being maritally related. The Church's sacramental activities should acknowledge partial growth and support further development. Perhaps the state's legal ceremony of marriage is not the time for the Church's main sacramental expression. Certainly the Church can no longer assume that a spiritually binding marriage exists because it has been physically consummated. People grow into union over a period of years. The sacrament ought to be expressed more fully at ten, twenty-five, or forty years of union. The couple may need sacramental support in the down period of the 30s or the midlife crisis at 40 more than on their wedding day.

This approach would further change the Catholic Church's outlook on divorce. Church concern for permanence in human commitment is admirable, but that concern has to be expressed within a developmental understanding of human life. Divorce can simply be a recognition of the fact that a growing commitment does not always reach a stage of permanence. If matrimony were thought to be a series of steps in everyone's life, then divorce would mean many different things. In some instances the Church might strongly resist divorce. In other cases divorce, even if not an event to celebrate, might still be seen as a healthy and holy step.

This attitude toward matrimony might provide support for people I have called "married singles," those who are maritally related but not rearing a family. The fact that they may wish to resist cultural myths or state controls could be supported by a form of matrimony. In an older theology the main purpose of marriage was said to be the procreation and education of children. A more liberal view has tried to raise the love of the spouses to a position of equal importance. What might make more sense is two distinct forms. Marriage has for millennia been directed toward family and perhaps should remain that way. For the millions of people who are sanctified by marital love but are not procreating/educating children, a different social form needs recognition. Eventually this form might include homosexual love, but that will take time to be explored.

B. Baptism/Confirmation/Orders

Modern Catholic theology which has incorporated New Testament and patristic study refers to the sacraments of initiation. What became baptism and confirmation were part of a ceremony (which together with the Eucharist) received the adult into the Church. In time baptism became a sacrament for infants while confirmation has been a ceremony rather awkwardly stuck into early adolescence. In recent times there have been various proposals to move confirmation to early adulthood, to reunite confirmation with baptism and to make adult baptism be the "norm."[28]

Much of this discussion is helpful though it needs a life-span context. Adult baptism as a "norm" does not mean that children should be excluded but that adulthood is the basis for rethinking church membership. Children might still be in the majority of those baptized. When a child is baptized, it can be a community celebration. A supportive community during pregnancy would mean that at birth the child has already entered an "adult community." The ceremony is an admission that willy-nilly the child is religiously stamped for life by parents and other adults.

What is needed, perhaps at the end of adolescence, is a further expression of baptism/confirmation when the young person would decide whether to become an adult member of the Church. Obviously that time cannot be rigidly fixed by age. There are complications in meshing Church practice and individual development, but the problem shouldn't be insuperable.

If baptism/confirmation were viewed this way, then a sacrament of orders might be an affirming of various Church roles.

Since early in its history The Church has seemed to have only one order: the ordained who do church work. Life-span theory would suggest a variety of steps and forms. Each order would be open to everyone, but it need not be supposed that there is only one route to go. The big problem is to break through the monolithic meaning of ordination in the Church which creates a clergy; all talk of "ministries" gets attached to the lay/clerical structure.

The spiritual and corporal works of mercy form a catalogue of possible Church ministries. Presiding at the Eucharist, visiting the sick, or teaching the young need not be part of one job. At the same time that the jobs are distinguished, each of them needs recognition and support by the whole Church. A person might be more inclined to the prophetic or teaching role in his or her 20s and more suited to the priestly role at 70. Work that requires aggressive organization might especially appeal to women in their 40s while a more nurturing job (e.g., youth counsellor) may be appropriate to 40-year-old men.

C. Reconciliation/Eucharist

These two sacraments are expressions of everyday life. Unfortunately, both have lost ground in Catholic lives. In the United States only one-half of Catholics attend Mass on Sunday and the great majority seldom or never go to Confession. The forms of each have changed over the past ten years but not sufficiently to meet the Catholic in his or her daily life. Both sacraments continue to reflect a church of clergy and laity rather than a community experience through diverse ministries.

A sacrament of being reconciled with one's parents, one's spouse, one's children, and oneself makes a lot of sense provided the setting is appropriate. A reconciling with the world and finally with one's sickness and death would also be integral to adult development. A reconciling with God is mediated through all those concrete expressions. The Catholic Church became bogged down on the question of age for first confession. The more meaningful question is the kind of rite appropriate for a child and various forms which a rite might have throughout life.

The Eucharist is the Church's central act in which it affirms the Jesus of the past, the presence of God in our midst, and the coming of Christ. This ritual can provide a sense of stability and continuity from the individual's early days to his or her final days on earth. The Eucharist can be a point of meeting for our family/community, our work and retreat. Concern for food and drink in a world where poverty and pollution are rampant needs sacramental support. Action for social justice needs to be rooted in the act of worship. By combining sacraments for crisis points and sacraments for daily activity the Catholic Church can provide a marvelous religious education for children and adults on their way to adulthood.

Notes

1. Jean Piaget and Barbel Inhelder, *The Psychology of the Child* (New York, Harper Torchbook, 1969).

2. Kohlberg has three levels: preconventional, conventional, postconventional. Each of the three has two stages: 1, Punishment and Obedience: the physical consequences of action determine its goodness or badness; 2, Instrumental Relativist Orientation: right action is what satisfies one's own needs; 3, Interpersonal Concordance of Good Boy/Nice Girl: good behavior is what pleases or helps others; 4, Law and Order: authority, fixed rule, social order; 5, Social Contract: right action is defined by individual rights and standards critically examined by the whole society; 6, Universal Ethical Principles: right is defined by decision of conscience in accord with self-chosen ethical principles appealing to logical comprehensiveness, universality, and consistency. See L. Kohlberg and R. Kramer, "Continuities and Discontinuities in Childhood and Adult Moral Development," *Human Development*, 12(1969), 93–120; also, Lawrence Kohlberg, "Education for Justice," in *Moral Education* (Cambridge, Harvard, 1970), 57–83.

3. For a similar criticism of Kohlberg's stages from a feminist perspective, see Carol Gilligan, "In a Different Voice: Women's Conception of the Self and Morality," *Harvard Educational Review,* 47(November, 1977), pp. 481–517.

4. E. L. Thorndike, *Adult Learning* (New York, Macmillan, 1928).

5. For a readable summary of studies on this point, see Paul Baltes and Warner Schaie, "The Myth of the Twilight Years," *Psychology Today*, March, 1974, pp. 35ff.

6. J. R. Kidd, *How Adults Learn*, rev. ed. (New York, Association, 1973), pp. 63f.

7. See John Horn, "Organization of Data on Life-Span Development of Human Abilities," in *Life-Span Developmental Psychology*, ed. Paul Baltes and K. Warner Schaie (New York, Academic, 1973), pp. 424–66.

8. G. Stanley Hall, *Senescence: The Last Half of Life* (New York, Appleton and Co., 1922).

9. Erikson, *Childhood and Society*, pp. 247–74.

10. Two major studies of adult development with longitudinal samples are: The Oakland Growth and Development Study begun at Berkeley in 1929 and The W. T. Grant Study begun at Harvard in 1938.

11. For an example of a scheme of adult development, see Gould, *op. cit.*

12. See Harvey Cox, "The Real Threat of the Moonies," *Christianity and Crisis*, November 14, 1977, pp. 258–63.

13. See David Moberg, "Religiosity in Old Age," in *Middle Age and Aging*, ed. Bernice Neugarten (Chicago, University of Chicago, 1968), pp. 497–508; Raymond Kuhlen, "Trends in Religious Behavior during the Adult Years," in *Wider Horizons in Christian Adult Education*, ed. Lawrence Little (Pittsburgh, University of Pittsburgh, 1962), pp. 1–26.

14. Barbara Fried, *The Middle-Age Crisis* (New York, Harper and Row, 1967), p. 59.

15. See Gail Sheehy, *Passages* (New York, Dutton, 1976), pp. 504–06.

16. Elisabeth Kubler-Ross, *Questions and Answers on Death and Dying* (New York, Collier, 1974), pp. 164–71.

17. See L. M. Stolz, *Influences on Parent Behavior* (Stanford, Stanford University, 1967); Maureen Green, *Fathering* (New York, McGraw-Hill, 1976), p. 159.

18. An exception to this rule is Angela Barron McBride. *The Growth and Development of Mothers* (New York, Harper and Row, 1973); see also Ann Oakley, *The Housewife, Past and Present* (New York, Pantheon, 1974).

19. Margaret Hennig and Anne Jardim, *The Managerial Woman* (Garden City, Doubleday, 1977).

20. See Bert Kruger Smith, *Aging in America* (Boston, Beacon, 1973), p. 156; Margaret Mead, "Grandparents as Educators," in *The Family as Educator*, ed. Hope Jensen Leichter (New York, Teachers College, 1974), pp. 66–75.

21. Elliott Jaques, "Death and the Mid-Life Crisis," *International Journal of Psychoanalysis,* 46 (1965), pp. 502–14.

22. See George Vaillant, *Adaptation to Life* (Boston, Little, Brown and Co., 1977).

23. Bernice Neugarten, *Personality in Middle and Later Life* (New York, Atherton, 1964), p. 192.

24. Maggie Kuhn, "Gray Panther Power," *Center Magazine*, March/April, 1975, p. 25.

25. Quoted in Ann Douglas, *The Feminization of Culture* (New York, Knopf, 1977), p. 140.

26. See Karl Rahner, *Meditation on the Sacraments* (New York, Seabury, 1977), preface: *Made Not Born* (Notre Dame, University of Notre Dame, 1976).

27. For some similar points on these rites by a Protestant educator, see John Westerhoff, "The Liturgical Imperative of Religious Education," in *The Religious Education We Need*, ed. James Michael Lee (Mishakawa, Religious Education Press, 1977), pp. 90ff.

28. See Ralph Keifer, "Christian Initiation: The State of the Question," in *Made Not Born* (Notre Dame, University of Notre Dame, 1976), pp. 140f.

7. Professionalism: Friend or Foe?

The preceding chapters have described the attempts to improve the education of adults in the Church and in the wider society. My approach has been to shift the burden away from the individual "adult educator" or church official toward the structural questions of contemporary organization. However, in trying to change the large organizations of our world we are faced with the big question: Where does one begin?

If one does not start at the right place and seize on the key issue, much effort can be wasted. Paulo Freire, writing from his experience in South America, stressed the need to first change the teacher-student relation in education. Instead of teachers and students, he wrote, we need communities of student-teachers and teacher-students. Although I readily agree on the desirability of that change, I do not think it comes first. The United States is at a different stage of educational evolution in which the primary problem is not the teacher's power over the students. Freire notes three times in *Pedagogy of the Oppressed* that if bureaucracy is what follows liberation, then freedom has not been gained.[1] Since the beginning of this century in the United States the bureaucratic pattern of churches, schools, and most other organizations has been a main obstacle to an "adult society." Organization that is hierarchic, bureaucratic, and class-biased has remained almost impermeable to criticism and intractable to change. Why do reform movements always seem to reinforce the patterns of bureaucracy?

I would like to propose in this chapter that at the heart of this issue is the concept of "professional." It is an idea that needs more historical studies and more systematic analysis of its present form. Since "professionals" control the language, it is almost impossible to find any words to criticize professionals and professionalism. The concept of professional is a historically complex one and it is today more ambivalent than might be assumed. Both religious and adult concerns in education are intimately tied to the future of professionalism.

My thesis is the following: The "professional educator" in the Church is in a crucial spot to improve the Church and to affect the larger society. To do so, however, he or she needs to know the ambiguity of professionalism. He or she also needs a way to resist the negative meaning of professionalism while using the positive meaning of professional. This stance depends on a team or community approach to being a professional. I will develop this material in two sections: first, a historical sketch of the meaning of professional; second, a description of the meaning of professional team that would respond to the ambiguity of professionalism.

1. History of the Professional

I recently read a book entitled *Religious Education in the Church*. It struck me that much of the book, especially Chapter 21 on forming parish councils and hiring a Director of Religious Education (DRE), would have a contemporary message for Catholic parishes. The only surprising thing is that the book was written in 1918.[2] The Director of Religious Education (or Coordinator) movement began in the Roman Catholic Church in the mid-1960s. Enormous hopes and sometimes impossible burdens have been placed upon the shoulders of that group of people in the Catholic Church. Catholic educators could surely profit from knowing some of the Protestant experience in this area.

The Catholic Church is in danger of inventing organization that has long existed. Of course, Catholics may do the job better, but they are not likely to do so if they don't know the successes and failures of other attempts. One should also note that Protestants do not always know their own history, either. A helpful book for this area is Dorothy Jean Furnish's *DRE/DCE: The History of a Profession*.[3] She begins her history at the beginning of this century. I would like to go back further into the roots of both the director of religious education and profession.

I think one might trace the director of religious education on these shores back to 1632. In that year the First Church of Boston hired the Rev. John Cotton to be in charge of education. The church debated whether there might be "divers pastors in the same church." The solution was to have a minister who teaches or instructs and a pastor who preaches or exhorts.[4] From the seventeenth to the twentieth centuries churches have regularly had someone who directed religious education. But the question will be asked, was that person a "professional"?

Dorothy Jean Furnish is insistent and repetitive on the job of DRE becoming a profession in the twentieth century. She may be right, but I am more interested in the origin and meaning of profession. I think the question might then be raised whether DRE ought to be a profession.

The idea of profession has its roots in the religious order of medieval Catholicism. A person professed vows or, more exactly, a person was professed in vows. The passive voice was used in the Middle Ages and is still used today in that organization. "To be professed" was to have special grace and knowledge. But since profession like vocation was received from God, the claim of profession was not self-serving.

The one who was professed had a corresponding responsibility. To be professed was to take a stand and to step before the group. The move required conviction, courage, and a willingness to sacrifice some individual comforts. One had to con-fess what one was pro-fessed in. The person was ready to be an advocate in the service of God and church. Profession was therefore a special knowledge dependent upon advocacy of one's beliefs.

Three learned professions developed around these ideals. Law, medicine, and divinity were "callings" that required dedicated service and special knowledge. The military life was sometimes conceived on the same lines. These "secular" professions inevitably shifted the concept toward a claim to status. The professional did not receive much money, but he was rewarded with symbols of achievement by the community. At the end of the Middle Ages the twin marks of "public proclamation" and personal discipline carried over from the religious use of the term.

The beginning of modern times saw an expansion of the professions and a narrowing in the areas of special knowledge. Instead of lawyers there were now barristers, solicitors, and attorneys. There was also a continuing shift from the "confession of faith" to the "possession of technique." Francis Bacon wrote in 1605: "Amongst so many great foundations of colleges in Europe, I find strange that they are all dedicated to professions, and none left free to Arts and Sciences at large."[5] This contrast between the professions and arts sciences is an ominous prefiguration of further splits in recent times.

The meaning of professional continued to shift toward the individual's status and reward. Being professional meant protecting an esoteric knowledge from the general public who would not understand such things. A professional was given "license" in the double sense of the word. The community gave approval for his moving without interference in his special domain. In return the professional was to be a man of service which meant that dedication to a client's interest took precedence over personal gain.

The United States in its colonial period trailed far behind Europe in the development of professions. The scarcity of institutions and the need for versatility delayed professionalization. There was no medical school in the colonies until 1765. In eighteenth-century Virginia only one out of nine doctors had a degree, medical learning being transferred through clergymen, teachers, and governors.

By our standards the colonies may seem primitive in their regard for "professional standards." They did not always view it that way. Describing his native Virginia in 1728, William Byrd said: "It was a place free from those three great scourges of Mankind: Priests, Lawyers and Physicians."[6] Another way to put it is that in the absence of a profession of lawyers every landowner became his own lawyer. The founding documents of the United States were framed in legal language that spoke to the literate community. In his famous speech on the American Colonies in 1775 Edmund Burke acknowledged that "in no country perhaps in the world is the law so general a study."[7]

The main story of professionalization in the United States lies in the nineteenth century. The newly developing middle class became entwined with the idea of professions. Before this time there had been "middling" people between upper and lower classes. The nineteenth century saw the growth of vertical groupings and a ladder of success. One had to get credentials and advance in one's profession. A successful professional life became the game to play for a vast population moving from agricultural to "service" jobs. The United States prides itself on not having any rigid social classes. Every little boy, it was said, could grow up to be President. The freedom to advance was also a burden and there was little cushioning for anyone who could not run the race.[8]

Divinity or ministry did not remain unaffected by the culture's emphasis on professional advancement. The minister might still say he had a calling, but he also had to worry about his career. "The profession of the ministry had entered a competitive society in which unrestrained individual self-determination undermined traditional life-styles."[9] The ministers still warned young men against "versatility" and "indecision of character," but their own careers increasingly reflected the mobility they condemned.[10] A clergyman's parish tenure in New Hampshire in 1790 averaged thirty years; by the 1830s it was four to eight years.[11]

In fairness to the clergy it should be noted that their mobility was not born mainly of greed. The clergy in the first half of the nineteenth century were in grave economic trouble. The clergyman was scrambling about for a new way to live in this professionalized society. Shouldn't the church have something valuable to contribute to the meaning of profession? One would think so, but the clergy seemed caught between an earlier meaning of calling, loyalty, and service and a modern conception of specialized skill.

To illustrate this problem I would cite professional athletics today. Perhaps one of the last professional groups to make the move from fifteenth- to nineteenth-century meanings is athletes. The problem is now hitting professional sport hard and in some sports more than others. Joe DiMaggio had a vocation to the Yankees; the New York stars of the 1970s have the Yankees as part of a career. Baseball has enough of nineteenth-century entrepreneurship in it to survive a grab for money and individualistic players. Football or basketball are more peculiarly of the twentieth century and are increasingly in trouble. They require some meaning of professional other than "loyalty to an order imposed by God" or an individual on the way up. What they need is a twentieth-century meaning of professional that would combine the best of the fifteenth and nineteenth centuries. Anyone interested in church professional work would do well to watch professional sport in the next decade.

The nineteenth century expanded the ways in which the individual could work toward the top and serve middle-class needs. Everybody was becoming a "professor" with his own niche. Burying the dead, for example, was made into a profession. There developed a language of casket, funeral homes, and funeral directors. The rural cemetery domesticated death and placed it in the hands of professionals. A profession supposedly polices itself and offers what the client needs and wishes. The funeral industry is not the only profession which causes suspicions that professional protections may be a cover for conspiratorial actions against the public.

Higher education was surprisingly slow in becoming professionalized, but when it arrived, it did so decisively. The university or college joined the route of the professions only late in the nineteenth century. Charles William Eliot, in his 1869 inaugural address at Harvard, complained that "it is very hard to find competent professors for the University. . . . The pay has been too low and there has been no gradual rise out of drudgery, such as may reasonably be expected in other learned callings."[12] Partly through Eliot's influence this picture of the university was soon to change and dramatically so. The reader need only ask: Where are all the "professors" now? The university took the divisive issues of society and defined them within the curriculum of the university.

Educators at primary and secondary levels were slower to professionalize and it might be debated whether school teaching ever did become a profession. The preparation of school teachers became linked into state governments rather than universities. Teaching became the woman's job (along with nursing). In 1841 the Boston School Committee said that it preferred women teachers because they are "unambitious, frugal and filial."[13] Those adjectives are almost the exact opposite of the meaning of professional developing at the time.

While the teachers may not have constituted a profession, a group of men did get much of the control of schools. At the end of the nineteenth century an explosion of "administrators" occurred. These people along with school boards constituted a powerful group that insisted on the word "professional" to describe themselves. At the turn of the century the National Educational Association supposedly represented teachers. But whereas the teachers were overwhelmingly female in number, the organization was almost entirely in male hands.[14] Beginning in 1916 (with the founding of the American Federation of Teachers) and increasingly in the latter half of the century, teachers turned to the labor union as a form of leverage and protection.

The twentieth century continued apace in the development of professions and a culture of professionalism. The university provided entrance into the professions which required more specialized knowledge and longer schooling. The professionalizing of the culture widened the split between social classes. Joseph Kett locates the turning point at 1880 when parents had to think of getting their children on the right track early in life. Prior to that, "youth of different classes had worked side by side on farms and in small machine shops, even though their ultimate destinations differed."[15]

The twentieth century was a time of narrower and more powerful skills. What was one profession in the nineteenth century might become ten in the twentieth century. "Progress" demanded this division and then added to it. Science wedded to technology provided miracles of industrial progress. However, there was a distressing flaw pointed to by A. N. Whitehead: "The discoveries of the nineteenth century were in the direction of professionalism, so that we are left with no expansion of wisdom and with greater need of it."[16] Whitehead's concern is an echo of

Bacon's three centuries earlier, but enormous changes had occurred in the interval. Wisdom as defined by Whitehead is "the fruit of balanced development." An absence of such wisdom in the twentieth century could have disastrous results in the form of war and ecological destruction.

What also awaited full development in the twentieth century was a worldwide stratification of rich and poor. The international order divides into the few who have the power to define problems and the masses of people who have their problems defined for them. "The poor are those whose plans never work out," in the definition of Barbara Ward.[17] In poor countries around the world there is an almost desperate interest in education. Literacy, books, and professional jobs appear to be a panacea. But poor people operate in a world already defined against them.

I would recall here some of the data in Chapter One of this book. With all of its good intentions the adult education movement seems constantly to add to the split between the class of professional and everyone else. The Report of the 1972 Adult Education Congress warned that the gap is widening. As poor countries try to go the route of professionalization, they lag far to the rear of rich countries. The most successful individuals are under pressure to become a new ruling class or to find their fortune in the so-called advanced world.

The ambiguity of professionalism reached some kind of culmination in the 1960s, but it is not clear what has been learned. In the mid-1960s an editor of a collection on professions could say that "the problem of the professions" is nothing less than the "problem of America." That may have been true but in a way not intended by this writer who thought that "because there are simply not enough professionals to go around, the practitioner of today is perforce burdened with too much work."[18]

At about that time in the 1960s Paul Goodman was teaching a course on "Professionalism" at the New School for Social Research.[19] To Goodman's astonishment the students distrusted and rejected all the professionals that Goodman brought into the course. He described the students as thinking that "it was necessary only to be human . . . and all else would follow. . . . Suddenly I realized that they did not believe there was a nature of things."[20] Goodman's conclusion may be correct here, but he makes a big jump from the data. Actually, the explanation may be simpler, namely, that the students objected to a culture based on a hierarchy of professions. Much of their opposition may have smacked of mindlessness and laziness, but they might still have had their sights on a real problem.

Goodman's conviction was confirmed by the fact that students rejected the professionals' admissions of wrongdoing in their professions. But the students' instincts may have been justified. Erik Erikson has said that a peculiarity of the academic mind is to think that recognition of a dialectic means that one has escaped the dialetic.[21] The professional person who admits and condemns corruption in his or her profession does not thereby escape the corruption. The admission of the problem is not itself sufficient because the main problem is not individual failure but the structure of the profession itself.

The problem is an extraordinarily difficult one and the rebels of the 1960s did not solve the problem. If a lawyer becomes aware of the ambiguities of a professional legal class, what can she/he do? Resigning from the law may salve the individual's conscience, but such action does not correct the bias built into the system. Reforms according to the rules of the profession are not likely to correct a class bias built into the existence of the profession. Where does one go? Part of the answer lies in recovering an earlier meaning of professional. We need people who act professionally in both the medieval and the modern sense. By working within their professions they may be able to subvert a culture based on professionalism.

Before describing this style of action a final word should be said in this historical sketch of directors of religious education. Furnish locates the beginning of the profession at the turn of this century. That period was a big one for the invention of professions and a time of shift for Protestant churches. The Sunday School was undergoing a period of severe criticism.

As would happen later in Catholicism, the DRE was to be the answer. "All we need is a trained professional." While it is easy to talk about professionals, it may be more difficult to find a profession to be in. The claim that Directors of Religious Education constituted a profession seems to be questionable, to put it mildly. There were no more than 150 such people by World War I and about 1000 by the end of World War II. They were located only in Protestant churches and most important, the job was ill defined even to the 1950s. A large number of Catholics entered the DRE ranks in the last decade. Whether there is yet a profession could be debated.

One change that is usually passed over quickly in Protestant literature is a change from Director of Religious Education to Director of Christian Education.[22] In most churches the job changed names, which is a highly significant fact. The term DCE has been practically unknown in Roman Catholicism so that DCE is an ecumenical obstacle to Catholics and more obviously to Jews and others who have a religious education interest.

The main point here is that Protestant professionals have tended to move away from the aegis of secular education and into closer relation with divinity or ministry. The entrance of women and men into a "ministry of education" gives the job of DRE/DCE greater status. Something similar may happen in the Catholic Church as DRE is a job more and more accepted in the Church.[23] The choice here should be looked at very carefully. The DRE may achieve professional status but at the expense of reinforcing a split between professional Church officials and the rest of the Church. While the DRE may be strongly pushed in this direction, other images and language should be explored before it is too late.

2. The Professional Team

Why, as exemplified by Furnish's book, are people so anxious to be part of a profession? The answer is obvious if one considers the alternatives. The opposites of professional are amateur and lay. The word "amateur" has roots in the eighteenth-century Enlightenment. Voltaire could describe himself as an amateur of wisdom with the word carrying a sense of enthusiasm and commitment. Perhaps that meaning can be recovered, but there is no doubt that in a world of professionals and amateurs today the amateurs are on the bottom. The other main word which contrasts with professional is "lay." Here the contrast is complete, the lay person doesn't play the game at all but instead is on the receiving end. A lay person is someone lacking in a particular skill or special knowledge.

This split between the meaning of professional and the meaning of lay is complete. It cannot be overcome by "upgrading the laity." Since there is no positive meaning of lay, there is nothing to build upon. By definition a lay person is someone who is deficient in something. The word provides no basis for creating a new relationship.

Anyone who doubts this fact might consider Sigmund Freud's attempt to create "lay analysts."[24] Freud was rightfully concerned that his theory of psychoanalysis would be taken over by the medical profession in the United States. He insisted that psychoanalysis could be practiced by a "layman," that is, one who did not go the route defined by the medical profession. What would have been more effective would have been a new model distinct from that of the medical. But Freud was already so enmeshed in the medical profession that he could not see his way clear of the categories of medical doctor and layman.

What I would propose here as a step forward is to distinguish between the words "professional" and "professionalism." The former has an almost completely positive meaning, but the latter is in large part negative. The opposite of professional is unskilled, incompetent, or ignorant. However, the opposite of a culture of professionalism is not necessarily a culture of unskilled and ignorant people. The opposite of a society composed of professional classes could be teams or communities of people, each of whom possesses some skills and the skills trained to varying degrees. Some of the newer professions might give up the pretense of being a profession and go back to being a useful job. The older professions might rediscover their pasts and undergo some radical change.

The medical profession provides an instructive illustration for anyone concerned with contemporary professions. Medicine is, of course, one of the oldest professions. However, the nineteenth century was the era of its great advancement to a place of unchallenged superiority in society. The attitude of the medical profession was reflected in its code of ethics drawn up by the American Medical Association in 1847. Article V, section 9, stipulates that "a wealthy physician should not give advice *gratis* to the affluent; because his doing so, is an injury to his professional brethren." Article VI, section 2, warns that "a peculiar reserve must be maintained by physicians toward the public in regard to professional matters."[25] Such statements defined a stance of the medical profession in the nineteenth century. The medical profession won its battle to become autonomous, but the victory may prove self-destructive. In the modern world a certain lack of knowledge may generate trust in the knowledgeable people, but complete ignorance of a subject so intimate as health can generate resentment, distrust, and irrational decisions.

The most obvious sign of the problem is money. Beginning in 1965 health costs simply went out of control. There are many factors involved here, especially the entrance of large amounts of government money into a structure not ready for it.[26] One element that has received much publicity is the rising cost of insurance for doctors. Malpractice suits and settlements were a symptom of the changed attitudes of patients, juries, and the general public. There is a crisis of money, but more deeply there is a crisis of confidence.

Another symptom of medicine's problem is the sexual division. More than 93 percent of doctors are men while more than 95 percent of nurses are women. An increasing number of women as doctors and more male nurses will probably help the profession. But the question that remains is whether there are two distinct roles, to doctor and to nurse, and how are they related. Why has the division of roles been along sexual lines? Is the "nurse practitioner" a concept that will break through the split of nurse and doctor?

While doctors and nurses work through their changing definitions of role, they cannot forget the public. The "patients" hold the final power in redefining the meaning of medical professional. New ways of involving everyone in his or her own health care is the job for the future. A modern form of first aid, for example, in treating heart failure, has to reach most if not all of the public. Popular writing that avoids both quackery and technical jargon is a great need.[27]

A fundamental change in the medical profession will take decades of effort. Some lines of direction, however, are already clear. The medical school has to prepare men and women who are ready to work in teams. Much of their learning has to be on-the-job training and continuing professional education. Perhaps most importantly the medical professional has to involve the patient in self-regeneration. The word "layman" ought to disappear and criticism should become more widespread but also more intelligent. Those who hold powerful positions in the medical profession may not like these directions. But even they may see that the alternative is to have ever growing financial problems at the top and increased medical charlatanry at the bottom.

When one turns from medicine to ministry, there is some bad news and some good news. The bad news is that the church is one of the originators of the paternal system that created a professional class (a clergy) and a laity. The good news is that the church is also a founder of the good meaning of professional, that is, the person who is dedicated to serving human needs with skill, advocacy, and courage. What has to be done is to recover a meaning of professional that is buried in church tradition and devise a form for it that will resist modern professionalism.

The church's problem runs parallel to the medical profession. The Christian clergy were as successful as doctors in creating a separate realm for themselves. "Ministry" as a name for church activity was also a name for the professional clergy. In the Roman Catholic Church the religious order might have been a third force, that is, men and women who were neither clergy nor laity. In practice, however, the men became clericalized and the women became a subprofession to the clergy. In the Catholic Church, therefore, "professional" has generally meant priests and nuns with a division of roles that resembles doctors and nurses.

In one respect the Church's problem is considerably more grave than that of the medical profession. However much someone may distrust doctors nearly everyone finally comes to them. Change is being forced upon the medical profession because doctors must work with sick people. In addition, people know what they want from medicine and usually they know when they have received it. Very little of that applies to church ministry. If people are fed up with the division of clergy and laity, they need not fight it. Many of them simply leave.

The Catholic Church's problem is signaled by the twin issues of clerical celibacy and the ordination of women. There is danger that these two symptoms may be mistaken for the disease. The Catholic Church has in obvious form what most contemporary institutions have in veiled fashion: a top stratum of individual males married to the profession. In one respect the Catholic Church is further behind, but if the need is to recover a past tradition the backwardness can be turned to advantage. Some of the dedicated men and women in the Church could experiment with new forms of brotherhoods and sisterhoods.

Ordaining women into what now exists as clergy is nowhere near radical enough. A married clergy that includes some women will reinforce the split between professional and lay. Here as elsewhere Catholics and Protestants could learn from one another and move toward what doesn't now exist in either church. Catholicism is stronger on the community side which needs recovery from the past; Protestantism often has a modern form of professionalization.

As with the medical profession what is most needed are teams of men and women who are ready to pool their respective professional skills. Within a church context those skills would include teaching, counseling, celebrating, and organizing. One should note here that many of the skills may not have names. In a culture of professionalism only those skills have names which are licensed or certified. A job for the religious organization is to resist that closure and to insist that there are more services and more human needs than have been dreamt of by college catalogue makers.

A church or parish today has a basic choice to make: It can continue to offer clergy services with occasional programs involving laity. Such a church is likely to serve a diminishing number of people with services that are either a duplication of services available elsewhere or are activities out of touch with the center of people's lives. The other route for a parish/church is one that would eventually eliminate both clergy and laity, replacing them with communities of people whose prayer and social action are at the center of life. No sensational proclamations are necessary or desirable. The route I describe is a long, patient journey that some churches have begun without fanfare. The need is for a change of language, imagery, and institutional form that requires the quiet, concerted, and dedicated activity of generations.

What can be done by the people who are the present church professionals? How do they help to move the church from a class-based bureaucracy to an organization of communities? Actually, the first thing may be to learn how *not* to do some things lest the important work remain with the professional class. However, they can take some definite steps, especially in creating models of cooperative teams. The exact mode of operation for the team can be discovered only on the building site, but I would suggest four principles that should be kept in mind.

1. The Professional Team Is at the Center, Not the Top

This point may seem small, but it is the indispensable step. A professional team has to imagine itself and speak of itself as forming a nucleus of service to a wider community. This sense of center ought to be reflected in physical ways as well. Professional facilities should be physically near the center. The design of a building ought to show the same outlook.

A new distinction of public and private is needed for persons who try to operate this way. Professional skill does need distancing from some feelings so that technical concentration becomes possible. In addition, workers need time and space for their own personal interests. Professionals in modern times have moved between the enclosed private space of the family and the defined public space in the bureaucracy. What would become possible for a professional team is a movement from periphery to center. There would be a continuum of involvement and standing back but not a radical separation.

2. Division of Tasks

A professional team would consist of people who have a variety of skills. Work has to be divided among the group, but the basis of division that immediately presents itself is likely to be an inadequate one. Since institutions have already categorized people in mechanical fashion, existing divisions will probably need resistance. For example, in educational work, age of recipients might seem to be the obvious way to divide the work. There are diocesan teams that have one person with young children, one with youth, one with young adults, and one with the old. Although that division is clear, there are other divisions that should be explored. Specifying tasks by age groups can unintentionally reinforce age segregation which is one of the main things to be resisted by a professional team. Instead of individuals who know stages of child, youth, and adult it might be preferable for one person to know psychological stages, another to be attentive to family/community issues, and a third person to be concerned with the schooling/work involvement of the clients.

What is likely to happen with such a team is that talents and needs emerge which do not have any names. Each job need not be fitted into a preexisting slot. Within a team an individual can be allowed to do and supported in doing whatever he or she does. Elisabeth Kubler-Ross tells of a woman who was influential in her own work.[28] The woman was a black cleaning lady in a hospital where Kubler-Ross was working with a professional team in caring for the dying. Kubler-Ross noticed that patients improved when this woman had been near them. Kubler-Ross eventually discovered unique abilities to help the sick which the woman had developed from her own experience. She was a professional toward the sick though she was being paid to clean floors.

Many things need doing which have no professional name. Work with infants, disabled people, and old people involves skills and dedication not available through license or diploma. A person becomes more and more professional in doing a job well. For example, an urban parish today with many old people may need someone to be a liaison between those people and city services. The person doesn't have to hold a degree in gerontology, but he or she does need patience, dedication, and organization. He or she also needs the communal support of professionals to work in a world that is anonymous but is still a place where people suffer and die.

3. Small Number

A professional team would ideally have more than two but not more than six or seven people. Two does not provide the necessary variety and flexibility; for a community two have to give birth to someone or something. Once the number goes above six or seven, a bond of mutuality among the members becomes practically impossible.

The purpose of the small group is not to be the "saved church" but to be a microcosm of church structure. Therefore, if the group is successful it does not follow that more people should be brought into it. Other small groups should be stimulated rather than have one group keep growing. All groups don't have to have the same level of professional sophistication. One person from the most highly professional group could be a catalyst for a new group.

4. Diversity

Any professional team has to be trying to break through the segregations which are part of a culture of professionalism. In a group of six or seven there cannot be representatives of every nation, race, religion, and age. Except as a last resort and only as a transitional tactic are quotas the answer. But a group can make immediate changes of language and begin to diversify.

Any church group should be able to achieve sexual integration quickly. A professional church team should include men and women in equal or near equal numbers. The women are not there to be secretaries or housekeepers but to share in the full range of responsibilities. A church team should also be able to get some spread of ages in the group and some non-academic types in the group. A full range of age, race, and ethnicity may take a long time to reach but can be moved toward with determined steps.

What is the role of the "professional educator" in a church professional team?[29] There is a task of education internal to the team and a different task in relation to other people and other institutions. The title of Director of Religious Education may not survive the change I am describing although I think the title is fairly accurate. The person who directs religious education is not teacher, administrator, or the program itself. Director describes a definite and positive task but allows for flexibility in doing the job. The competing name in Roman Catholic circles, coordinator, is also a good name, but it ought to be coordinator of religious education and not "parish coordinator."

The professional educator has a responsibility to educate the other members of the team. That job has to be undertaken cautiously so that the process is not abrasive and thereby self-defeating. Nonetheless, there has to be someone in particular who reminds the group of its inevitable tendency toward sex, age, and other forms of bias. The professional educator ought to be constantly aware of the language, imagery, and institutional form of the team. Adult education programs in parishes often become the domain of an intellectual elite. The professional educator ought to be constantly reminding the team that the education of all adults in the parish is a central task of the parish.

External to the team, the professional educator has two distinct roles. One is to relate to institutions of education outside of a church context. The educator in the church is not simply a church minister. He or she needs a foot inside the university, local government, or private agencies. The professional educator's commitment is not 100 percent to the existing church. The church educator precisely for the good of the church has to stand against the church in the name of education. This stance, too, should not be sharply abrasive, but it should be crystal clear. The way educators can contribute to the Church is to resist ecclesiastical language and not allow the institution to swallow them. The swallowing is done with the best of intentions and it does relieve the tension, but the Church will have lost a crucial lever for its own advance.

Toward the rest of the people who form the Church the educator's job is to involve as many people as possible. People drift away from the Church because nothing really involves their energies. Or they have worked hard and there seemed little appreciation of their efforts. A hierarchy of jobs exists in many churches and when people have gone up the rungs they sometimes disappear. The educator's best instrument is probably a direct invitation by mail, phone, and in person. "Do you want to do a job that is specific but which will be designed with your help?" That question will get a better response than a sign on the bulletin board saying that teachers are needed for Sunday School or CCD.

People are understandably hesitant to present themselves as teachers ready for a classroom of youngsters. However, there are many people who would like to play the role of teacher within a group in which everyone has a job and everyone is helped to do the job. Here the lack of professionalism can actually be an advantage. Professional teachers sorely need cooperative teams, but few schools have moved much in that direction. Individualism and isolation have been integral elements in the attempt to make school teaching a profession.[30]

Church groups are free to invent their own forms of teaching and learning by drawing upon the experience, knowledge, and unnamed skills of the members. The director's job is to structure a situation which allows the emergence of many teachers in a community and to provide the back-up assistance as it is needed.

What the church would be demonstrating by an organization of communities is that people can govern their own lives and that every person has some talent to contribute to the governing. The worldwide educational revolution that is needed must be educational in nature if it is to open new routes for the poor as well as the rich. The principle of Edmund Burke remains valid: "Everything ought to be open but not indifferently to every man (and woman)."[31] Everyone is not equal in all ways, but all people can participate with the talents God has given them.

Notes

1. Paulo Freire, *Pedagogy of the Oppressed* (New York, Herder and Herder, 1970), p. 43.

2. Henry Cope, *Religious Education in the Church* (New York, Scribner, 1918).

3. Dorothy Jean Furnish, *DRE/DCE: The History of a Profession* (Nashville, United Methodist, 1976).

4. See Rutman, *op. cit.*, p. 107.

5. Quoted in Robert Jay Lifton, *The Life of the Self* (New York, Simon and Schuster, 1976), p. 166.

6. See Daniel Boorstin, *The Americans: The Colonial Experience* (New York, Random House, 1958), p. 189.

7. *Ibid.*, p. 201.

8. For the whole nineteenth-century period in the United States, see Burton Bledstein, *The Culture of Professionalism* (New York, Norton, 1976).

9. *Ibid.*, p. 174.

10. See Kett, *op. cit.*, pp. 104f.

11. See Douglas, *op. cit.*, p. 28.

12. Bledstein, *op. cit.*, p. 274.

13. Quoted in David Tyack, *The One Best System* (Cambridge, Harvard, 1974), p. 60.

14. See *Ibid.*, p. 265.

15. Kett, *op. cit.*, p. 152.

16. Alfred North Whitehead, *Science and the Modern World* (New York, Macmillan, 1937), pp. 282f.

17. Barbara Ward, *The Home of Man* (New York, Norton, 1976), p. 229.

18. Kenneth Lynn, *The Professions in America* (Boston, Houghton Mifflin, 1965), p. xi.

19. Paul Goodman, *New Reformation* (New York, Vintage, 1970), pp. 47–63.

20. *Ibid.*, p. 48.

21. Erik Erikson, *In Search of Common Ground* (New York, Norton, 1973), p. 108.

22. Furnish, *op. cit.*

23. For a similar analysis of the Catholic experiment with the diaconate, see John Moriarity, "Neither Priest nor Layman," *Commonweal*, May 21, 1976, pp. 331ff.

24. See Freud, *op. cit.*; for a similar criticism, see Torrey, *op. cit.*

25. Quoted in Bledstein, *op. cit.*, p. 192.

26. See Victor Fuchs, *Who Shall Live?* (New York, Basic, 1974).

27. For a good example of the writing needed, see Norman Cousins, "Anatomy of an Illness as Perceived by the Patient," *Saturday Review*, May 28, 1977, pp. 4ff.

28. See the movie "Death and Dying" done on Kubler-Ross's work produced by NBC television.

29. For a study of the DRE role, see Maria Harris, *The DRE Book* (New York, Paulist, 1976).

30. See Dan Lortie, *Schoolteacher* (Chicago, University of Chicago, 1975), p. 237.

31. Quoted in Nisbet, *op. cit.*, p. 239.

Conclusion

When people become aware of the need for some large-scale change, the inevitable question is: Where do I begin? The answer in this book has been twofold: 1) a person can immediately begin changing the way he/she speaks about education, religious education, and adulthood; 2) he/she can demonstrate at least in microcosmic fashion another model of education. These two things go together: One learns to speak more precisely as one works at new models of action.

The educational needs of adults in the Church cry out for a more adequate language of description and more effective programs. The strange twist is that directly concentrating on adults as an isolated problem may not be the best way to serve adult needs. A description that opposes adult and child is not the best one; a language that separates adult and parent is a dangerous one.

Programs that are intergenerational would be helpful to children, youth, younger adults, and older adults. Programs that affirm parenthood as an exalted role of adulthood, though only one role of adulthood, would affirm all adults.

Religious education is not under the control and direction of Christian churches. There are numerous settings in which religiously educational activity occurs. Nonetheless, Christian churches, if they are ready to accept what seems a more modest role than they claimed in the past, could make a great contribution to education and religious education. Churches have to cooperate with each other and also with other educational and religious institutions of the twentieth century.

In a recent *New York Times* there was an interview with a German film maker who said: "I think Christianity is a great thing but all the churches should be blown up." That kind of flippant cynicism has always done well in the United States. But he is dead wrong. If I had to use the same terms, I would reverse the saying: Christianity, as a vague ideology to which most people 'give lip service, needs "blowing up." In contrast, local churches have the greatness of existence. Despite their past and present problems, they have a concreteness that makes action possible. Churches retain an investment of trust and a possibility of acting when no one else is there. The religious education that helps us all toward adulthood is a project worthy of the continued effort of churches.